Test Your Baseball Literacy

R. Wayne Schmittberger

D0063976

John Wiley & Sons, Inc.
New York • Chichester • Brisbane • Toronto • Singapore

Library of Congress Cataloging-in Publication Data

R. Wayne Schmittberger
    Test your baseball literacy/R. Wayne Schmittberger
        p.   cm.
    Includes index
    ISBN 0-471-53622-9 (pbk. : alk. paper)
     1. Baseball   2. United States   3. Miscellanea   I. Title.
    GV867.3.S35   1991
    796.357.0973   dc20   90-19369

Printed in the United States of America
91 92 10 9 8 7 6 5 4 3 2 1

Preface

In writing a book of this kind, the easy part is finding enough material for questions. What's hard is narrowing it down.

More than any other sport, baseball lends itself to statistical "games within a game." For fans, poring over box scores to see how their favorite players are doing is still fun long after the division race has been decided. For managers and general managers, the numbers help decide who should play or whether to make a certain trade. For players, records can be worth small fortunes when it's time to negotiate a new salary, and bonuses are sometimes conditioned upon reaching specific levels in certain statistical categories.

The importance of keeping good baseball records was realized early in the game's history. As a result, nearly a century and a quarter's worth of raw data has been compiled and then used to determine batting averages, runs batted in, earned run averages, and dozens of other statistics.

Now, in the age of computers, statistics are proliferating. New, sometimes complex measures of performance are touted as being far more accurate measures of a player's true value to his team than "old-fashioned" statistics such as batting average or RBIs. Now, if we wish, we can check to see how a player has batted against fastball pitchers on Tuesday night games played on artificial turf with men in scoring position. And for every new statistic, a dozen new names are liable to start appearing in record books: the single-season leader in each league, the record for reaching a certain level in the most consecutive years, the lifetime leader, the leader by position or handedness—and it goes on and on.

Many records, of course, are arbitrary. I'm thinking of those that are cast in terms of numbers that have special meaning only because we, as a species, happen to count in tens. Is driving in 100 runs in a season significantly better than driving in 99? Why is a pitcher who has won *more than* 20 games in a season commonly referred to as a "20-game winner"? And when we talk about the number of years in which a player hit more than a certain number of home runs, why do we always pick a total such as 30 or 40 home runs, instead of, say, 32, as we might if (like a computer) we counted by twos or sixteens?

The truth is that whatever numbers we choose as milestones will be arbitrary. Fortunately, it doesn't matter. All we are trying to do by establishing a performance ladder with well-defined rungs is to give ourselves a way to organize some of baseball's voluminous information into a more coherent form. It's much easier to remember who the 20-game winners and .300 hitters were last year than to recall each of their exact numbers. And as long as we find our approximations useful in comparing players or teams—and experience indicates that we do—it makes no difference that our ladder's rungs were placed some arbitrary distance apart.

By now you may be wondering whether all 20 quizzes in this book are devoted entirely to statistics. Far from it. As central as statistics are to baseball, there's a lot they don't tell.

Even if you are a long-time baseball fan, you may be surprised at how much you don't know about the game's history. Learning about the people that have shaped the game, and about such things as the changes in rules and equipment that have helped the game continue to evolve and prosper, can provide a much deeper appreciation of the way baseball is played today.

The book covers other baseball topics, too, ranging from minor leagues to player salaries, and from baseball films to baseball cards. And five of the quizzes (Chapters 1, 6, 11, 15, and 20) are of the potpourri variety, where you'll find questions on just about any baseball subject you might think of.

All the questions in the book are multiple choice, with a single correct answer. But the answers go beyond—sometimes far beyond—a simple "A," "B," "C," or "D." Most questions call for at least a brief explanation or elaboration, and some answers beg new questions. When I've piqued the reader's curiosity, I've tried to satisfy it.

Player statistics are complete through the beginning of the 1991 season. A handful of questions refer to records that could possibly change before the book gets in to some readers' hands, but this has been avoided wherever possible.

I would like to thank Paul Dixon for his helpful advice, and Robert Davids for lending his expertise and making many valuable suggestions on the manuscript.

May you enjoy taking the quizzes as much as I enjoyed creating them.

—R.W.S.

Contents

Chapter 1

Batting Practice

This warm-up quiz includes a little of everything: hitting and pitching statistics, baseball history and rules, and curious facts and anecdotes. The emphasis is on the basics, but there are definitely some questions that may throw you a curve. (Answers and explanations begin on page 7.)

1.1 Since 1977, what have the covers of baseballs been made of?
A. cowhide
B. horsehide
C. pigskin
D. plastic (artificial animal hide)

1.2 What is the greatest number of consecutive batters ever to reach base safely in a major league game?
A. 10
B. 15
C. 20
D. 25

1.3 Of the 12 players making at least $3 million a year in 1990, how many were in the All-Star Game that year?
A. none
B. 4
C. 8
D. 12

1.4 For many years, the number 714 was very familiar to fans as Babe Ruth's record home run total—a record broken in 1974 by Hank Aaron. Aaron's new record total may not yet be as well known. Exactly how many home runs did Aaron wind up with?
   A. 715
   B. 733
   C. 755
   D. 795

1.5 Lelands is a New York-based auction house, world-renowned for selling fine sports memorabilia. In 1990, at Lelands's twelfth major auction, a mint-condition Babe Ruth autographed baseball sold for about how much?
   A. $100
   B. $1,000
   C. $10,000
   D. $100,000

1.6 Which of these team relocations happened first?
   A. The A's moved from Philadelphia to Kansas City.
   B. The Browns moved from St. Louis to Baltimore, becoming the Orioles.
   C. The Boston Braves moved to Milwaukee.
   D. The original Washington Senators moved to Minnesota, becoming the Twins.

1.7 The major league record for the most home runs in a season is, of course, 61 (by Roger Maris in 1961). But what is the record for the most *doubles* in a single season?
   A. 47
   B. 57
   C. 67
   D. 77

1.8 Upon which of these occurrences does an umpire *not* give a hand or arm signal to indicate what has happened?
   A. ball
   B. foul ball
   C. out
   D. safe

1.9 Besides the American and National Leagues, four other leagues were recognized by the Special Baseball Records Committee in 1968 as having been "major leagues." Which of these major leagues was in existence in this century?
   A. American Association
   B. Federal League
   C. Players' League
   D. Union Association

1.10 Legally, a pitcher's glove may be which of these colors?
   A. gray
   B. green
   C. red with blue stripes
   D. white

1.11 Who holds the career record for striking out the most times?
   A. Bobby Bonds
   B. Reggie Jackson
   C. Dave Kingman
   D. Babe Ruth

1.12 What broadcaster was the first to become famous for the home-run call, "That ball is going, going…gone"?
   A. Mel Allen
   B. Red Barber
   C. Howard Cosell
   D. Phil Rizzuto

1.13 Who among these players was *not* a switch-hitter throughout his major league career?
   A. Lou Brock
   B. Eddie Murray
   C. Red Schoendienst
   D. Reggie Smith

1.14 What's the smallest number of pitches a pitcher can throw and still get credit for a complete game—assuming the game is not shortened for any reason and does not end in a tie?

A. 24
B. 25
C. 27
D. 28

1.15 When St. Louis Browns owner Bill Veeck signed a midget, Eddie Gaedel (3′ 7″) in 1951, Gaedel walked on four pitches in his only plate appearance. Why didn't Gaedel ever play another game?

A. The league president banned him from baseball.
B. He got a better offer from a traveling circus.
C. He was dropped from the roster after the game because Veeck never intended to use Gaedel as more than a one-time publicity stunt.
D. He was injured sliding when he tried to steal second base.

1.16 How has the strike zone's vertical range been defined since 1969?

A. from the armpit to the bottom of knee
B. from the armpit to the top of the knee
C. from the top of the shoulder to the bottom of the knee
D. from the top of the shoulder to the top of the knee

1.17 Who holds the career record for pitching the most complete game shutouts?

A. Grover Cleveland Alexander
B. Walter Johnson
C. Christy Mathewson
D. Nolan Ryan

1.18 Willie Mays made the "Catch" in the same park where "Shot Heard Round the World" was made three years earlier. Where?

A. Candlestick Park
B. Ebbets Field
C. The Polo Grounds
D. Yankee Stadium

1.19 What is the term for imaginary leagues in which competitors simulate the drafting of real players, trade and cut them from their teams as in real baseball, and then get points or dollars based on their players' real-life statistical performances throughout the baseball season?
  A. Armchair
  B. Beer & Pretzel
  C. Couch Potato
  D. Rotisserie

1.20 When was the 1,000,000th major league run scored?
  A. 1926
  B. 1951
  C. 1976
  D. It has not yet happened, but is most likely to occur in the year 2001.

1.21 Which infielder generally wears the smallest glove?
  A. first baseman
  B. second baseman
  C. shortstop
  D. third baseman

1.22 According to American League rules, which of these statements about designated hitters is *false*?
  A. The DH may become the pitcher in the middle of the game.
  B. The DH named in the starting lineup must come up at least one time, unless the opposing club changes pitchers.
  C. A manager may choose not to use a DH and let his pitcher bat for himself throughout the game.
  D. A DH removed for a pinch hitter may reenter the game in another capacity, provided he never came to bat.

1.23 What team was originally known as the "Innocents"?
  A. Phillies
  B. Pirates
  C. Red Sox
  D. Yankees

1.24 Joe Sewell set a record for playing the most consecutive games without striking out. How many games in a row did he avoid whiffing?

    A. 38
    B. 68
    C. 98
    D. 115

1.25 Who was the first baseball player to appear on a U.S. postage stamp?

    A. Ty Cobb
    B. Lou Gehrig
    C. Jackie Robinson
    D. Babe Ruth

Answers and Explanations

1.1 **A. cowhide** Until 1975, baseball rules required that ball covers be made of horsehide—and they were. But that year, as horsehide was growing scarcer, the rules changed to allow ball covers to be made of either horsehide or cowhide. About the same time, the A.G. Spalding Company (Chicopee, Mass.), which had been the exclusive major league supplier of baseballs since 1877, announced that it would no longer manufacture baseballs after 1976, because it was no longer profitable for them. Rawlings Sporting Goods (St. Louis), which had occasionally made baseballs for A.G. Spalding as a subcontractor during the previous few years, began to supply balls to the major league balls in 1977, using only cowhide. When the Rawlings balls were introduced in 1977, pitchers, hitters, and scientists carefully compared their performance to that of the old balls. For the most part, they did not find significant differences.

1.2 **C. 20** Boston accomplished this against Detroit on June 18, 1953, in the seventh inning. The National League record is 19, done just once in this century—by Brooklyn against Cincinnati, on May 21, 1952, in the first inning.

1.3 **B. 4** The four were Jose Canseco and Rickey Henderson of the A's, Will Clark of the Giants, and Kirby Puckett of the Twins. Dave Stewart of the A's would probably have been on the team, but for a reported agreement between him and his manager—Tony La Russa, who was also manager of the American League squad—to skip the game because it would interfere with his normal pitching rotation. Other $3 million men who missed the game were Joe Carter of the Padres, Eric Davis of the Reds, Mark Davis of the Reds, Mark Langston of the Angels, Don Mattingly of the Yankees, and Paul Molitor and Robin Yount of the Brewers.

Incidentally, of the 25 players who were eligible

for free agency and signed for $1 million or more in the previous off-season, only three were on an All-Star team: Neal Heaton of the Pirates, Rickey Henderson, and Dave Parker of the Brewers.

1.4 **C. 755**   If 733 sounds familiar, it's Aaron's National League total, all hit for the Braves from 1954-74. He also hit 22 home runs in two years in the American League, for the Milwaukee Brewers, in 1975-76. In 23 years, his home run total never fell short of double figures, and his personal high was 47, hit in 1971. Ruth hit his 714 home runs for the Red Sox, Yankees, and Braves from 1914-35.

1.5 **C. $10,000** $9,983, to be exact. Usually, Ruth-autographed baseballs in good condition can be expected to fetch between $3,000 and $5,000. Balls signed by Lou Gehrig are worth a similar amount.

1.6 **C. The Boston Braves moved to Milwaukee.**   The Braves moved to Milwaukee after the 1952 season. The Browns moved to Baltimore after the 1953 season, and the A's to Kansas City after 1954. The Senators were in Washington through 1960; when they moved to Minnesota, a new Washington expansion team took their place. The second Washington team moved to Texas after the 1971 season, becoming the Rangers.

1.7 **C. 67**   Earl Webb set this record in 1931, playing for the Boston Red Sox, but it was something of a fluke: In no other season did he have more than 30 doubles. The National League record for doubles in a season is 64, achieved by Joe Medwick while playing for the St. Louis Cardinals in 1936. Unlike Webb, Medwick was an outstanding doubles hitter throughout his career; he had 40 or more doubles seven years in a row (1933-39), followed by four more consecutive years with at least 30. George Burns also hit 64 doubles for Cleveland in 1926.

1.8 **A. ball**   An umpire indicates a foul ball by extending an arm and pointing toward foul territory with one of the fingers on the hand of that arm. An "out" is indicated by sticking up a thumb, and a "safe" call by extending arms in opposite directions. (Umpires show a strike by pointing a finger up.) Different umpires often have distinctive styles of gesturing, but they all follow these basic patterns.

1.9   **B.   Federal League**   The Federal League existed from 1914-15, and attracted many ballplayers from the American and National Leagues. Dates of the other leagues are: American Association, 1882-91; Players' League, 1890; and Union Association, 1884. The National League goes back to 1876 and the American League to 1901.

1.10   **B.   green**   A pitcher's glove may be any solid color except white or gray. The reason for this rule is to ensure that the pitcher's glove does not become a distraction to the batter as he looks for the pitch.

1.11   **B.   Reggie Jackson**   Jackson struck out 2,597 times, playing for Kansas City, Oakland, Baltimore, the New York Yankees, and California from 1967-87. In second place is Willie Stargell (Pittsburgh, 1962-82) with 1,935 strikeouts, followed by Mike Schmidt (Philadelphia, 1972-89) with 1,883. For many years, Babe Ruth held the record with 1,330. Mickey Mantle broke that record in 1964, but more than 30 players now have higher strikeout totals than Ruth.

1.12   **A.   Mel Allen**   The famous broadcaster, who was known as the "Voice of the Yankees" from 1939-64, is also remembered for other famous lines, such as his exclamation "How about that!"—originally uttered when Joe DiMaggio got a hit after returning from a bone spur injury. Allen, along with Red Barber, was inducted into the Hall of Fame in 1978 for his work as a broadcaster. To the generation who grew up in the 1980s, he is known as the narrator of the TV show *This Week in Baseball*.

1.13 **A. Lou Brock**   Brock, who played from 1961-79 for the Cubs and Cardinals, was once a switch-hitter (prior to which, reportedly, he had been purely a righthanded hitter). By the time he reached the big leagues, he had given up righthanded hitting entirely, because his great speed allowed him to beat out many more infield hits batting a step closer to first base. Ty Cobb apparently became a lefthanded hitter for the same reason.

1.14 **B. 25**   He would throw the fewest pitches in an eight-inning complete-game effort. This means that he would have to be on the visiting team—and his team would have to lose—so that the game would be over before he pitched the ninth inning. One way to throw just 25 pitches would be to give up a leadoff home run and then retire the next 24 batters on a single pitch each, losing 1-0.

1.15 **A. The league president banned him from baseball.** Veeck was very upset by the ban, instituted by American League president Will Harridge, since the baseball rules did not specify any minimum height. Veeck suggested he might retaliate by demanding a ruling on whether Yankee shortstop Phil Rizzuto (listed as 5'6") was a short ballplayer or a tall midget.

1.16 **B. from the armpit to the top of the knee**   Actually, the rule doesn't specify "armpit." It gives the upper range as the point that is midway between the top of the shoulder and the top of the pants. But although this location varies according to the batter and how he crouches while swinging, it is usually equivalent to the armpit. In practice, though, umpires rarely seem to call strikes higher than the waist (why is one of baseball's great unsolved mysteries). The 1969 rule replaced the 1963 rule, which defined the range as the top of the shoulder to the bottom of the knee.

1.17 **B. Walter Johnson**   Johnson had 110 (all for Washington, 1907-27). Alexander is second with 90 (for the Phillies, Cubs, and Cardinals, 1911-30), and

Mathewson is third with 83 (Giants and Reds, 1900-16). Eddie Plank's 64 (Athletics, St. Louis Terriers of the Federal League, and Browns, 1901-17) is the record for a lefthander. Entering the 1991 season, Ryan's total (Mets, California, Houston, and Texas, 1966-present) is 59.

1.18 **C. The Polo Grounds** The Polo Grounds. The "Shot" was Bobby Thomson's ninth-inning, three-run homer off Ralph Branca of the Brooklyn Dodgers, which clinched a pennant in the third and deciding game of a three-game playoff in 1951. Mays made the catch in the first game of the 1954 World Series against Cleveland, on a no-out fly by Vic Wertz with runners on first and second, and the score tied 2-2. He caught the ball over his shoulder about 460 feet from home plate. The Giants went on to win the game and sweep the series.

1.19 **D. Rotisserie** Rotisserie League baseball, which is named for a former Manhattan restaurant where the original participants met, began around 1980. In just a decade, Rotisserie Leagues have developed several hundred thousand followers. They have also been responsible for the formation of dozens of statistical services, as well as expansion of space given to statistics by newspapers.

1.20 **C. 1976** For the record, it was scored by Bob Watson of Houston, on May 4, 1976 against the Giants—assuming, of course, that the previous 999,999 runs were accurately counted.

1.21 **B. second baseman** The smaller size makes it easier to pivot quickly and remove the ball in the middle of a double play. Joe Morgan used one of the smallest gloves of any player in the last few decades; it was so small that it would fit inside many other infielders' gloves. Under baseball rules, first basemen are allowed to wear larger gloves than anyone except a catcher—and they usually do.

1.22 **D.** **A DH removed for a pinch hitter may reenter the game in another capacity, provided he never came to bat.** Once replaced, the DH is out of the game for good, like any other player.

1.23 **B.** **Pirates** The Pittsburgh club of the 1890 Players' League was known as the Innocents because of their weak performance, winning only 23 games and losing 113. When they joined the National League in 1891, they gained a reputation as "pirates" when they stole a player named Lou Bierbauer, a fine defensive second baseman, from Philadelphia. Bierbauer had jumped from Philadelphia to the Players' League in 1890; but instead of rejoining his former team when the new league collapsed in 1891, he was switched to Pittsburgh because of a clerical error. Pittsburgh kept him, and the name "Pirates" stuck.

1.24 **D.** **115** Sewell was not fanned in 437 at bats, for the Cleveland Indians, May 17 through September 19, 1929. During his career he struck out just 114 times in 7,132 at-bats.

1.25 **C.** **Jackie Robinson** A commemorative stamp was issued in 1982, the tenth anniversary of Robinson's death. Debuting in 1947 as the first black player in the major leagues in the twentieth century, Robinson paved the way for all black players since. Thus, his effect on the game has been incalculable.

Chapter 2

Once Upon a Game

Baseball is a relatively young game, but already its history is replete with colorful characters, outrageous incidents, and hard-to-believe forgotten rules. The fact that the game keeps evolving makes definitive comparisons between players of different eras all but impossible—but allows good-natured debates to go on forever. (Answers and explanations begin on page 19.)

2.1 Although the early history of baseball is not fully known, who is now generally given credit for inventing the game?
- **A.** Alexander Cartwright
- **B.** Abner Doubleday
- **C.** Iroquois Indians
- **D.** A.G. Spalding

2.2 Before nine-inning baseball games became standard in 1857, what did a team have to do to win?
- **A.** be ahead after five innings
- **B.** be ahead after seven innings
- **C.** be first to score nine runs
- **D.** be first to score 21 runs

2.3 Which was *not* a team in the 1871 National Association?
- **A.** Cincinnati Red Stockings
- **B.** Cleveland Forest Citys
- **C.** Fort Wayne Kekiongas
- **D.** Troy Haymakers

2.4 Defensive play was revolutionized when Bill Doak's fielder's glove was introduced by Rawlings Sporting Goods company of St. Louis. In contrast to the old "pancake" glove, it had a pocket that could be adjusted by means of leather laces. What year was this glove introduced?
   A. 1880
   B. 1900
   C. 1920
   D. 1940

2.5 Which of these major league rules was adopted more recently than the other three?
   A. foul bunts counting as strikes
   B. foul balls other than bunts counting as strikes
   C. four balls constituting a walk
   D. infield fly rule for one-out pop-ups

2.6 When did major league annual attendance first total more than 5 million?
   A. 1884
   B. 1904
   C. 1924
   D. 1944

2.7 In its early days, the American League was able to lure away National League stars because the National League had a salary cap. What was the most a National League player could officially make in 1901?
   A. $24 per game
   B. $240 per game
   C. $2,400 for the season
   D. $24,000 for the season

2.8 Christy Mathewson is usually credited with the invention of the "fadeaway." What is this kind of pitch called today?
   A. curveball
   B. forkball
   C. screwball
   D. spitball

2.9 From what word did the term baseball "fan" derive?
  A. "fan," because Wrigley Field bleacher seat spectators would fan themselves with newspapers in the hot summer afternoons
  B. "fanatic," describing the extreme enthusiasm of certain spectators
  C. "fanfare," referring to the blare of trumpets that audiences would bring to games in the early years
  D. "fanny," referring to the part of the anatomy that spectators get the most use from during a game

2.10 Why were St. Louis Browns manager Jack O'Connor and coach Harry Howell barred from major league jobs after the 1910 season?
  A. They bet on horses.
  B. They conspired to rig the season's batting title.
  C. They insulted the league president in a newspaper interview.
  D. They were arrested for demonstrating against the sale of alcohol at ballparks.

2.11 Why did the Red Sox owner Harry Frazee sell Babe Ruth and other star players?
  A. to finance Broadway plays
  B. to pay taxes he owed the government
  C. to raise money to buy a Caribbean island
  D. to rid himself of players he considered too greedy

2.12 In 1893 the pitcher's mound was moved to 60 feet 6 inches from home plate (measuring from the edge of the pitching rubber to the back of home plate). What was the distance just before the change?
  A. 40 feet
  B. 50 feet
  C. 60 feet
  D. 70 feet

2.13 Who was the first president to attend a major league baseball game while in office?
  A. Calvin Coolidge
  B. Benjamin Harrison
  C. Theodore Roosevelt
  D. William Howard Taft

2.14 What year was the spitball abolished—with exceptions
for a few veteran spitball pitchers who were allowed to
throw it for the remainder of their careers?
  A. 1900
  B. 1910
  C. 1920
  D. 1930

2.15 Of these four league presidents, which one served in the
National League?
  A. Joe Cronin
  B. Ford Frick
  C. William Harridge
  D. Ban (Byron) Johnson

2.16 When was the first major league baseball game broadcast
over the radio?
  A. 1901
  B. 1911
  C. 1921
  D. 1931

2.17 Who introduced night baseball and commercial air travel
to the major leagues, and offered to trade Joe DiMaggio
for Ted Williams?
  A. Andy MacPhail
  B. Larry MacPhail
  C. Lee MacPhail
  D. Waddy MacPhail

2.18 Which of these players was still active after the others'
playing careers were over?
  A. Ty Cobb
  B. Rogers Hornsby
  C. Christy Mathewson
  D. Cy Young

2.19 As far as is known, admission was first charged at a baseball game at Fashion Race Course on Long Island, New York, in 1857, for a game between All Star New York and Brooklyn. How much did it cost?
   A. 5 cents
   B. 25 cents
   C. 50 cents
   D. 1 dollar

2.20 Since what year have the rules prohibited players from leaving their gloves on the field while going in to bat?
   A. 1894
   B. 1914
   C. 1934
   D. 1954

2.21 Who was Bowie Kuhn's immediate predecessor as baseball commissioner?
   A. Happy Chandler
   B. General William "Spike" Eckert
   C. Ford Frick
   D. Peter Ueberroth

2.22 When did the American League first use the designated hitter rule?
   A. 1968
   B. 1973
   C. 1978
   D. 1983

2.23 When did the current sacrifice fly scoring rule, under which a batter is not charged for a time at bat, go into effect?
   A. 1894
   B. 1914
   C. 1934
   D. 1954

2.24 Why did Cincinnati leave the National League in 1881?
   A. The league objected to their players' salary structure.
   B. They wanted to play Sunday games and sell beer at their park.
   C. They were too much better than the other teams in the league.
   D. They were too much weaker than the other teams in the league.

2.25. Who was the first free agent?
   A. Curt Flood
   B. Catfish Hunter
   C. Dave McNally
   D. Babe Ruth

Answers and Explanations

2.1 **A. Alexander Cartwright**   The popular notion that Civil War major general Abner Doubleday invented baseball originated in 1907, when a committee was commissioned to look into the history of the game. Committee chairman A.G. Mills, at the urging of Albert Spalding, wrote the committee's report crediting Doubleday—with whom Mills had served in the Army—with having invented the game in 1839. The trouble was that the report had Doubleday playing baseball in Cooperstown, New York, at a time when he was in fact a West Point cadet. Major league baseball reinforced the legend in the 1930s, when it used the Mills report as the basis for its heavily promoted 1939 centennial celebration and the location of its new Hall of Fame.

In reality, baseball-like games had been evolving throughout the early 1800s, and were played by many different sets of rules. When the Knickerbocker Baseball Club of New York was formed in 1845, it asked Alexander Cartwright to standardize the rules. Cartwright's rules included establishing the diamond-shaped field, the division of fair and foul territory, and nine player positions; fixing the distance between successive bases as 90 feet; and eliminating the making of putouts by throwing the ball at a runner (ouch!). Cartwright's grandson presented evidence of Cartwright's contributions in 1938. As a result, Doubleday was never enshrined in the Hall of Fame, and Cartwright was. (See, however, the answer to question 2.2.)

Cartwright went to California during the Gold Rush in 1849 (as a result, knowledge of baseball reached the Far West surprisingly early), then moved to Hawaii, where he worked for many years as a banker and also served as Honolulu's fire chief.

2.2 **D. be first to score 21 runs**   The other team did get "last licks," though. Until 1990, baseball historians thought that the first documented modern baseball

game (i.e., played under Cartwright's rules) was
played on June 19, 1846, in Hoboken, New Jersey,
between Cartwright's Knickerbockers and the New
York Nine (the final score was 23-1 in favor of the
Nine, in four innings). But in 1990, Edward L.
Widmer, a Harvard graduate student, found a
newspaper record from *The New York Morning News,*
describing a game played on October 21, 1845. That
game, too, was played in Hoboken, but the teams
were the New York Ball Club and the Brooklyn
Players. The final score, 24-4 in favor of New York,
suggests that the 21-run rule was in effect and casts
some doubt on how many of the rules attributed to
Cartwright actually originated with him.

But even if Cartwright's "official" rules were
simply selections from rules that already existed, his
contribution to the game was still very significant.

2.3 **A. Cincinnati Red Stockings**   The Cincinnati Red
Stockings were charter members of the National
League, which was formed in 1876. The National
Association, officially recognized by the Special
Baseball Records Committee as the first professional
league (though not as a major league), started in 1871
with nine teams: the Boston Red Stockings, Chicago
White Stockings, Cleveland Forest Citys, Fort Wayne
Kekiongas, New York Mutuals, Philadelphia
Athletics, Rockford Forest Citys, Troy Haymakers,
and Washington Olympics.

2.4 **C. 1920**   The original model had just three laces for
webbing and a very small pocket, but it kept evolving
into more modern-looking gloves.

2.5 **B. foul balls other than bunts counting as strikes**
The rule that foul balls other than bunts count as
strikes was adopted by the National League in 1901
and by the American League in 1903. Foul bunts had
counted as strikes since 1894, and the number of balls
needed for a walk had been reduced several times (in
1880, for example, it was reduced from nine to eight),
but it finally went down to four in 1889. The infield

fly rule went into effect for one-out situations in 1895, and was extended to no-out situations in 1901.

2.6 **B. 1904**   In 1904, with a schedule of 154 games, American League attendance was 3,024,028 and the National League's was 2,664,271. The previous year, the combined attendance was about 4,700,000 for a 140-game schedule.

2.7 **C. $2,400 for the season**   Many players, however, received under-the-table compensation, given to keep them from jumping leagues.

2.8 **C. screwball**   Mathewson, who pitched from 1900-16, mostly for the New York Giants, would only throw a few screwballs per game, but the extra pitch was definitely part of his success. His career was so outstanding (373 wins, 188 losses, and a lifetime 2.13 ERA) that he was one of the first five players elected to the Hall of Fame.

2.9 **B. "fanatic," describing the extreme enthusiasm of certain spectators**   Manager Ted Sullivan of the St. Louis Browns (the team that was renamed the Cardinals in 1899, not the later American League club of the same name) coined the term in 1883 after team owner Chris von der Ahe called the club's followers "fanatics." The term "fan" soon replaced the older term "krank."

2.10 **B. They conspired to rig the season's batting title.**   On the final day of the season, Nap Lajoie of Cleveland was in a close batting race with the highly unpopular Ty Cobb. During a doubleheader between St. Louis and Cleveland, O'Connor and Howell instructed rookie third baseman Red Corriden to play deep at third each time Lajoie came to bat. This allowed Lajoie to go 8-for-8 by beating out several bunts (a St. Louis outfielder also "lost" a ball of Lajoie's in the sun). Despite the gifts to Lajoie, Cobb was thought to have won the title anyway, by the slim margin of .385 to .384; but in 1981, *The Sporting*

News discovered that an error had been made in calculating Cobb's average that year—a game in which he had gone 2-for-3 had been counted twice, and he had really hit only .383. The matter quickly came before Baseball Commissioner Bowie Kuhn, who ruled that the error would not be corrected and that Cobb's 1910 batting title would stand.

2.11 **A. to finance Broadway plays**   Frazee was a theatrical producer who, during his ownership of the Red Sox from 1917-23, would sometimes sell star players to raise cash he needed for his plays. For selling Ruth to the Yankees, he received $100,000 in cash plus a $300,000 loan. Other star players he sold to the Yankees included Carl Mays, Herb Pennock, and Everett Scott. After Frazee's time, the Red Sox never again won a World Series, while the Yankees went on to win a record number of them.

2.12 **B. 50 feet**   The principal reason for the change was Indianapolis pitcher Amos Rusie ("The Hoosier Cannonball"), whose fastball reportedly ranked among the all-time best. (According to one story, the distance was supposed to have been increased to exactly 60 feet—in 1881, it had gone from exactly 45 to exactly 50—but a surveyor's error added 6 inches more.) The center of the pitcher's mound is now exactly 59 feet from the back of home plate, with the rubber located 18 inches farther from home than the mound's center.

2.13 **B. Benjamin Harrison**   Harrison saw a game between Cincinnati and Washington on June 6, 1892. Better known is the fact that on April 14, 1910, Taft became the first president to throw out the first ball of the season, in a game between the Washington Senators and the Philadelphia Athletics. Taft made it into an annual event.

2.14 **C. 1920**   In December 1920 it was agreed that all bona fide spitball pitchers then remaining in the National and American Leagues be exempted from the rule during the remainder of their major league careers. Eight from

the National and nine from the American were affected.
Burleigh Grimes was the last recognized spitball hurler
when he left the majors in 1934.

2.15 **B. Ford Frick**   Frick served from 1934 to 1951.
Johnson was the first president of the American
League, serving from 1901-27. Harridge (1931-59)
and Cronin (1959-73) were also American League
presidents.

2.16 **C. 1921**   On August 5, 1921, Harold Arlen broadcast a
game between the Pirates and Phillies over KDKA in
Pittsburgh. The Pirates won the game 8-5.

2.17 **B. Larry MacPhail**   Larry MacPhail was a
controversial—though often successful—baseball
executive with Cincinnati (1934-36), Brooklyn
(1938-42), and the New York Yankees (1945-47). The
DiMaggio-for-Williams deal was reportedly planned
while MacPhail and Red Sox owner Tom Yawkey
were out drinking; Yawkey apparently thought better
of it the next day. In theory, such a deal might have
helped both clubs, since it would have given
lefthanded-hitting Williams a short rightfield fence to
aim at in Yankee Stadium, while righthander
DiMaggio would have had the short—though very
high—leftfield fence in Fenway Park to go for. In
practice, though, while DiMaggio did hit far more
home runs on the road than at home, Williams usually
hit more at home.

   Larry MacPhail's son Lee served as president of the
American League from 1974-83, and Lee's son Andy
later became general manager of the Minnesota Twins.
(There has never been a Waddy MacPhail in baseball—
though a player named Waddy MacPhee appeared in
two games for the New York Giants in 1922.)

2.18 **B. Rogers Hornsby**   Hornsby was active from 1915-37
(Cardinals, Giants, Braves, Cubs, and Browns); Cobb,
from 1905-28 (Tigers and A's); Mathewson, from
1900-16 (Giants and Reds); and Young, from
1890-1911 (Cleveland, St. Louis, and Boston in the

National League; Boston and Cleveland in the
American).

2.19 C. 50 cents   Half a dollar was, of course, a significant
sum in those days.

2.20 D. 1954   In fact, though, most players had abandoned
the habit of leaving their gloves on the field long
before 1954.

2.21 B. General William "Spike" Eckert   Eckert served
from 1965-68. The post was vacant for a few weeks
until Kuhn was elected. Chandler was commissioner
from 1945-51, and Frick from 1951-65. Ueberroth
was Kuhn's successor, and served from 1984-89.

2.22 B. 1973   The rule was adopted in 1973 as an experiment;
it was made a permanent rule in December 1975. Nearly
all leagues at all levels of competition now use the DH
rule, except, of course, the National League. There are
signs, however, that the American League is seriously
reconsidering the rule.

2.23 D. 1954   The rule has been altered a number of times in
the history of the game.

**2.24 B. They wanted to play Sunday games and sell beer
at their park.**   When the National League banned
both beer and Sunday games, Cincinnati switched to
the more liberal American Association in 1882. They
returned to the National League for good in 1890, at a
time when competition from the rival Players'
League caused severe, ultimately fatal financial
pressures for the American Association.

2.25 B. Catfish Hunter   Hunter was freed from his contract
with the Oakland A's for the 1975 season by
arbitrator Peter Seitz, because A's owner Charlie
Finley failed to pay a bonus required by the contract
($50,000 that was to go into a life insurance fund).
Hunter soon signed with the Yankees for $3.5
million, ushering in an era of free agency and high
salaries.

Chapter 3

So You Thought You Knew the Rules...

Though they seem second nature to most of us who have grown up playing the game, baseball's rules are really rather complicated. Just try explaining to, say, a foreigner who has never seen baseball played, but who reaches first base in your pickup softball game, something as simple as how far he should run—or whether he should run at all—if the next batter makes contact with the ball.

Even for devoted fans, though, there are many rules that come up seldom enough to be puzzling when they do. Occasionally, a situation can even stump the umps and make them reach for their copies of the official rules. Here's a quiz that test how much you *really* know about how the game is supposed to be played. (Answers and explanations begin on page 32.)

    3.1 Approximately how much should an official baseball weigh?
      A. 5 ounces
      B. 8 ounces
      C. 11 ounces
      D. 14 ounces

3.2 Approximately how big around is an official baseball?
  A. 5 inches
  B. 7 inches
  C. 9 inches
  D. 11 inches

3.3 Which of these bats would be legal to use in a major
league game?
  A. a 40-inch-long, 40-ounce bat, the lower 20 inches of
    which are covered with tape
  B. a 40-inch-long, 50-ounce bat, the lower 15 inches of
    which are covered with tape
  C. a 50-inch-long, 40-ounce bat, the lower 10 inches of
    which are covered with tape
  D. a 35-inch-long, 35-ounce bat painted bright blue,
    with no tape

3.4 A first baseman may wear a glove or mitt that is a
maximum of 12 inches long and 8 inches high. What
other defensive player could legally wear a
maximum-size first baseman's glove?
  A. catcher
  B. outfielder
  C. pitcher
  D. third baseman

3.5 Which of the following may appear on a uniform?
  A. a commercial emblem
  B. a picture of a baseball
  C. polished metal buttons
  D. tape of a color matching the color of the uniform

3.6 What is the shortest allowable distance for an outfield
fence?
  A. There is no minimum.
  B. There is no minimum for any one field, but the
    average distance from home to the fences must be at
    least 300 feet.
  C. 250 feet
  D. 300 feet

3.7 How high above the playing field is the highest point on the pitcher's mound?
A. 5 inches
B. 10 inches
C. 15 inches
D. 20 inches

3.8 Suppose the visiting Royals, trailing the White Sox 2-0 after six innings, score three runs in the top of the seventh inning. In the bottom of the seventh, the first two White Sox batters make outs; but before anyone else can bat, play is stopped because of snow. What happens to the game?
A. The game counts as a tie, and must be replayed in its entirety.
B. The game is treated as a suspended game, and must be continued from the exact point at which it was left off.
C. The Royals win 3-2.
D. The White Sox win 2-0.

3.9 For a game to be a "suspended game," which is picked up from where it left off, it must have gone at least regulation length (five innings, or four-and-a-half if the home team is ahead) if play was interrupted for which of the following reasons?
A. a curfew imposed by law
B. darkness when because of any law, the lights may not be turned on
C. failure of automatic tarpaulin equipment
D. light failure

3.10 Which of these statements is *false*?
A. If a batter is hit by a pitch in the strike zone, but made no attempt to avoid being hit, it is a strike.
B. If a batter is hit by a pitch in the strike zone, the pitch is a strike even if the batter did attempt to avoid being hit.
C. If a batter is hit by a pitch out of the strike zone, but made no attempt to avoid being hit, he is awarded first base.
D. If a batter is hit by a pitch out of the strike zone, but did attempt to avoid being hit, he is awarded first base.

3.11 Hitting which of the following things in fair territory will make a batted ball dead?
  A. a batting helmet accidentally dropped by a runner going from first to second
  B. a batting helmet deliberately thrown by a runner
  C. a piece of a broken bat
  D. the second base umpire, after the ball has ricocheted off the second baseman's glove

3.12 Suppose the sixth batter in the batting order is due to bat first in the bottom of the seventh inning. Instead, the seventh batter in the lineup comes up. No one notices the error, and he gets a single. The eighth batter in the lineup then steps into the batter's box. Before any pitches are thrown to him, however, the catcher realizes the batting order mistake and notifies the umpire. What happens?
  A. The batter who just stepped into the box is out, since he is the one who is batting when the mistake is noticed.
  B. The batter who was supposed to have come up sixth is out because he failed to take his turn.
  C. The runner on first is out for having batted out of turn.
  D. Nothing, because the team on the field did not notice the mistake in time.

3.13 With runners on first and second and no one out, the batter hits a chopper toward the second baseman. The runner on first accidentally slips and falls in the path of the ball, which hits him and then ricochets back in the path of the batter running to first. The batter doesn't notice the ball, and trips over it before reaching first base, kicking the ball into the dugout. The runner from second crosses the plate while the ball is in the dugout. What happens?
  A. Both players hit by the ball are out; the runner who scored must go back to third.
  B. Only the first runner hit by the ball is out; the runner who scored must go back to second.
  C. Only the first runner hit by the ball is out; the runner who scored must go back to third.
  D. Only the first runner hit by the ball is out, and the run scores.

3.14 In which of these situations is a batter who swings and misses at strike three automatically out?
   A. There are runners on first and second with two outs, and the catcher drops the ball.
   B. There are runners on first and third with no outs, and the catcher drops the ball.
   C. There are runners on second and third with one out, and the catcher drops the ball.
   D. With no outs and no one on base, the third strike hits the umpire on the fly, and the catcher catches it before it hits the ground.

3.15 If a pitched ball sails past the catcher and gets stuck in the home plate umpire's mask, how many bases may a runner advance?
   A. none
   B. one
   C. two
   D. as many as he can take before being tagged out by either the ball (once it is pried loose) or by the mask, which the umpire must allow the defensive team to use to tag the runner

3.16 If a game ends in a forfeit, what is the official final score?
   A. There is none.
   B. 1-0
   C. 9-0
   D. 1-0 in the American League, 9-0 in the National League

3.17 According to the ground rules of the Metrodome in Minneapolis, what happens if a ball hits a loudspeaker in foul territory, ricochets into fair territory, and is caught by a defensive player before it hits the ground?
   A. It is a fair, live ball, treated as if it had hit a fence; therefore, catching it does not make the batter out.
   B. It is a foul ball that becomes dead as soon as it hits the speaker; the batter continues to bat, and no runners may advance.
   C. It is a foul fly out, and runners may tag and advance at their own risk.
   D. The batter is out, but no runners may advance.

3.18 With no outs and runners on second and third, the batter
hits a sharp ground ball to the third baseman, who throws
the ball home a little too quickly, enabling the runner to
reverse course and get back to third. Before he gets back,
however, the runner from second slides into third. The
third baseman tags both runners while they are standing
on third. Who is out?
  A. both runners
  B. the runner from second only
  C. the runner from third only
  D. whichever runner is tagged first

3.19 With two strikes on the batter and a runner on third, the
runner tries to steal home. He gets a very good jump, but
is hit by the pitch, which is in the strike zone, as he
crosses the plate standing up. The batter strikes out
looking—but does the run score?
  A. no, regardless of the number of outs
  B. no, unless there were already two outs before the play
  C. yes, unless there were already two outs before the play
  D. yes, regardless of the number of outs

3.20 With the score tied in the bottom of the ninth, and the
bases loaded, the batter hits a line drive that bounces into
the centerfield stands on one hop. How many runs score,
and what is the batter credited with?
  A. One run scores, since that's all that's needed to end
  the game; the batter gets credit for a single.
  B. One run scores, but the batter gets credit for a double.
  C. Two runs score, and the batter gets credit for a double.
  D. Three runs score, and the batter gets credit for a
  double.

3.21 If there are runners on second and third, which of the
following constitutes a balk by the pitcher?
  A. faking a throw to second, and not throwing anywhere
  B. faking a throw to second, then throwing to third
  without stepping toward third
  C. faking a throw to third, then stepping toward second
  and throwing there.
  D. faking throws to both second and third, and not
  throwing anywhere

3.22 If there are runners on first and third, which of these acts does *not* constitute a balk by the pitcher?
  A. dropping the ball
  B. faking a throw to second base while standing on the rubber
  C. stepping toward second base and throwing there without standing on the rubber
  D. stepping toward third base and throwing there while standing on the rubber

3.23 If a fielder throws his glove at a fair ball and knocks it down, how many bases may runners advance?
  A. none, because it's perfectly legal
  B. one if the ball was thrown, three if the ball was batted
  C. two if the ball was thrown, three if the ball was batted
  D. two, regardless of whether it was a batted ball or a thrown ball

3.24 Of the nine defensive players on the field, how many must be in fair territory when the ball is pitched?
  A. at least one
  B. at least five
  C. exactly eight
  D. all nine

3.25 Which of the following does *not* require that a team play the rest of the game without a designated hitter?
  A. having a pinch hitter hit for any batter, and then enter the game as a pitcher
  B. switching a pitcher from the mound to a defensive position
  C. putting the DH into a defensive position
  D. replacing the DH with a pinch runner

Answers and Explanations

3.1 **A. 5 ounces**   Since 1872, the rules have specified that balls must weigh between 5 and 5.25 ounces.

3.2 **C. 9 inches**   Since 1872, the rules have specified that balls must be between 9 and 9.25 inches around.

3.3 **B. a 40-inch-long, 50-ounce bat, the lower 15 inches of which are covered with tape**   Bats cannot be longer than 42 inches, nor wider than 2.75 inches, but there is no restriction regarding weight. No more than 18 inches of the bat may be covered with such things as tape to help a batter improve his grip. Bats must be made of one or two pieces of wood, and must have a natural wood color. Dark natural wood stains are acceptable, but colors are not. The longest bat ever used in the major leagues may have been Al Simmons's 38-inch bat, and the shortest, "Wee" Willie Keeler's 30.5-inch one.

    The 18-inch rule was at the heart of the 1983 "pine tar" incident, in which George Brett hit a two-run, two-out, ninth-inning home run for Kansas City against the Yankees, apparently putting the Royals ahead by a run, only to be called out by the umpires when Yankee manager Billy Martin pointed out that Brett had more than 18 inches of pine tar on his bat. On appeal, the decision was reversed by league president Lee MacPhail, who said that Brett's penalty should have been limited to having his bat removed from the game. The home run counted, the game was picked up (weeks later) from the point of Brett's home run, and the Royals won.

3.4 **A. catcher**   Catchers are allowed to wear any kind of glove or mitt not more than 15.5 inches long, and not more than 38 inches in circumference. All fielders other than catchers and first basemen are limited to gloves with fingers—not fingerless mitts—with a maximum width of 7.75 inches. At one time, catchers could wear gloves of any size; the current size limitation was made a rule in 1965, as a reaction to Orioles' catcher Gus Triandos's use of a 45-inch-around mitt to catch knuckleballer Hoyt Wilhelm.

3.5 **D. tape of a color matching the color of the uniform** Tape of a color *different* from the color of the uniform is prohibited. The emblem is prohibited because of a rule against undue commercialization; pictures of baseballs are prohibited because of their potential to cause confusion; and polished metal and glass buttons are disallowed, too, probably because of the bright reflections they can cause, if not also because of their potential to cause injuries.

3.6 **C. 250 feet**   Although 250 feet is the officially allowable minimum, ball parks constructed after June 1, 1958 are required to have minimum fence distances from home plate of 325 feet down the lines and 400 feet in centerfield.

3.7 **B. 10 inches**   The highest point, of course, is the rubber, which is 18 inches farther from home plate than the center of the 18-foot-diameter pitcher's mound. From a point six inches away from the rubber, in the direction of home plate, the mound is supposed to slope down at a rate of one inch per foot.

3.8 **B. The game is treated as a suspended game, and must be continued from the exact point at which it was left off.**   But if the Royals had not scored, or had scored just one run in the top of the seventh, the White Sox would have won the game. And if the score had been *tied* after five or more complete innings, and the game been called during an inning in which the visiting team had *not* scored (or in which both teams had scored an equal number of runs, with the home team still batting), the game would have been a tie—meaning that all statistics would count, and the game would have to be replayed in its entirety.

3.9   **A. a curfew imposed by law**   If a game is called on
account of curfew (or weather) before it goes the
minimum regulation distance, it does not count and
must be completely replayed. But games called
because of equipment failure or darkness (e.g., if a
law prevented the lights from being turned on for
some reason) are continued from the exact point at
which they left off, regardless of the inning.

3.10 **C. If a batter is hit by a pitch out of the strike zone,
but made no attempt to avoid being hit, he is
awarded first base.**   A ball that hits the batter in the
strike zone is always a strike. When a pitch is thrown
out of the strike zone, the batter must try to avoid
getting hit; otherwise, it will only count as a ball, and
he will not be awarded first base.

3.11 **B. a batting helmet deliberately thrown by a runner**
Not only is the ball dead after hitting a deliberately
thrown helmet, but the baserunner who threw the
helmet is out for interference. A ball is in play if it
hits a broken bat or an accidentally dropped batting
helmet. And although a batted ball that hits an umpire
is dead, one that first hits a fielder and then hits an
umpire (or that hits a fielder and then a runner) is in
play.

3.12 **B. The batter who was supposed to have come up
sixth is out because he failed to take his turn.**   As
long as no pitches have been thrown to the next
batter, there is still time for the defensive team to
appeal to the umpire, and it is the batter who failed to
bat in turn who is out. This is an "appeal play": The
umpire is not allowed to call the infraction to
anyone's attention, and the defensive team must point
it out to take advantage of the mistake. In the
example in the question, if a pitch is thrown to the
eighth batter in the lineup, it is too late for any
appeal, and the game proceeds normally, with the
eighth batter continuing to bat, followed by the ninth,
and so on, according to the correct batting order.

3.13 **C. Only the first runner hit by the ball is out; the runner who scored must go back to third.** When a runner is hit by the ball, three things automatically happen: That runner is out, the ball is dead, and other runners (including the batter) advance one base. Since the ball was dead as soon as it hit the first runner, the fact that it hit the batter as he ran to first had no effect on the play.

3.14 **B. There are runners on first and third with no outs, and the catcher drops the ball.** With a runner on first, a batter is automatically out on a third strike, even if the catcher fails to catch the ball, unless there are two outs. Catching the ball off the umpire is not a valid catch; so in the situation in choice D, the catcher would have to tag the batter or throw the ball to first before the batter gets there to get him out.

3.15 **B. one** The ball is dead, but runners advance one base. The same rule covers balls stuck in catchers' masks or other parts of an umpire's uniform.

3.16 **C. 9-0** Forfeits may only be declared by the umpire in chief, but they may arise for any number of reasons, such as failure to remove an ejected player or failure to begin play when ordered to do so.

3.17 **C. It is a foul fly out, and runners may tag and advance at their own risk.** It counts as a foul fly out, and runners may tag and advance at their own risk, as on any other foul fly out.

3.18 **B. the runner from second only** The runner on third, not being in a force situation, has the right to stay there. In an infamous incident on August 15, 1926, *three* Brooklyn Dodger runners actually wound up at third base at the same time in a game against the Boston Braves. With the bases loaded, Babe Herman hit a long fly that bounced off the rightfield wall at Ebbets Field. The runner on third scored, but Dazzy Vance, the runner on second, hesitated once to see whether the ball would be caught and hesitated again rounding third. Then he retreated to third, just as the

runner originally on first was arriving, with Herman
close behind.

3.19   **C.   yes, unless there were already two outs before the
         play**   With fewer than two outs, the run would
         count; with two outs, it would not.

3.20   **B.   One run scores, but the batter gets credit for a
         double.**   The only situation in which more runs than
         the winning run can score in the last of the ninth or in
         the bottom half of an extra inning is with a home run.
         Until 1920, even home runs that drove in the winning
         run ahead of them were scored only as singles,
         doubles, or triples, according to how many bases the
         baserunner needed to advance to score the winning
         run. Originally, in 1968, the Special Baseball Records
         Committee voted to restore home runs to players who
         had lost credit for them this way, but the committee
         changed its mind in 1969.
            In 1931, a rule was added that when a player drives
         in the winning run in the bottom half of the final
         inning, the official scorer should credit the batter with
         however many bases the hit was likely to be worth. In
         the case of a ground rule double, there's only one
         possible ruling.

3.21   **B.   faking a throw to second, then throwing to third
         without stepping toward third**   A pitcher may fake
         a throw to second or third (but not to first—that
         would be a balk). After a fake, he may fake or throw
         to another base, but must step toward any base to
         which he actually does throw.

3.22   **C.   stepping toward second base and throwing there
         without standing on the rubber**   While standing on
         the rubber, a pitcher may not fake a throw to an
         empty base, nor throw to any base other than home.
         Dropping the ball with runners aboard is also a balk.

3.23   **C.   two if the ball was thrown, three if the ball was
         batted**   In addition, the ball stays in play, so that the
         runner—who is assured of a triple—may try to score
         at his risk. A similar rule applies if a fielder uses a

cap, mask, or other object to knock down a ball. Note, however, that if a fielder throws his glove up and knocks down a ball that would otherwise have left the park, the hit is ruled a home run.

3.24 **C. exactly eight**   The catcher must be in the catcher's box, which is in foul territory. All the other players must start in fair territory.

3.25 **D. replacing the DH with a pinch runner**   If the designated hitter is replaced with a pinch runner, the runner becomes the new DH.

Chapter 4

Through the Years

How meaningful are career records in baseball? Does a player who was fortunate to stay healthy long enough to play for 20 complete seasons deserve more recognition than a player whose career was bright but relatively brief?

In fact, lifetime records are very highly regarded by most baseball fans, and also by the sportswriters who elect players to the Hall of Fame. One reason is that to have even a chance to set most career records, a player needs to be active for a long time—and that won't happen in the big leagues unless the player is consistently playing very well. And even among players who are blessed with as much durability as skill, only the best earn a place in the career record books. (Answers and explanations begin on page 43.)

4.1 It is well-known that Pete Rose broke Ty Cobb's record for most career hits. But after Rose and Cobb, who stands third on the all-time hits list?
A. Hank Aaron
B. Stan Musial
C. Tris Speaker
D. Carl Yastrzemski

4.2 In what category did Babe Ruth and Hank Aaron end up exactly tied during their careers?
A. doubles
B. runs
C. runs batted in
D. total bases

4.3 Who had the most career home runs without ever having led a league in home runs during any season?
A. Jimmy Foxx
B. Reggie Jackson
C. Harmon Killebrew
D. Stan Musial

4.4 Among 300-game-winning pitchers, who has the best won-lost percentage?
A. Grover Cleveland Alexander
B. Lefty Grove
C. Walter Johnson
D. Cy Young

4.5 Among 300-game-winning pitchers who are no longer active, who had the *worst* won-lost percentage?
A. Steve Carlton
B. Phil Niekro
C. Gaylord Perry
D. Early Wynn

4.6 Who holds the record for the most career pinch-hit home runs?
A. Smoky Burgess
B. Cliff Johnson
C. Jerry Lynch
D. Graig Nettles

4.7 Who has the record for hitting the most home runs as an outfielder?
A. Hank Aaron
B. Willie Mays
C. Frank Robinson
D. Babe Ruth

4.8 Who holds the National League career record for most bases on balls?
A. Joe Morgan
B. Stan Musial
C. Mel Ott
D. Pete Rose

4.9 Who holds the major league career record for the most bases on balls?
- **A.** Mickey Mantle
- **B.** Babe Ruth
- **C.** Ted Williams
- **D.** Carl Yastrzemski

4.10 How many times was Hank Aaron walked intentionally during his career?
- **A.** 93
- **B.** 293
- **C.** 493
- **D.** 693

4.11 Who had the highest "walk average" (i.e., the highest ratio of walks to the sum of walks and at-bats) over the course of his career, among players with at least 5,000 at-bats?
- **A.** Richie Ashburn
- **B.** Mel Ott
- **C.** Babe Ruth
- **D.** Ted Williams

4.12 Who holds the record for the most extra-base hits in a career?
- **A.** Hank Aaron
- **B.** Stan Musial
- **C.** Babe Ruth
- **D.** Ted Williams

4.13 What is the major league career record for sacrifice flies?
- **A.** 121
- **B.** 221
- **C.** 321
- **D.** 421

4.14 Who is fourth—behind the almost legendary Cy Young, Pud Galvin, and Walter Johnson—in total innings pitched in a career?
- **A.** Steve Carlton
- **B.** Phil Niekro
- **C.** Warren Spahn
- **D.** Don Sutton

4.15 Who was the first major leaguer to pitch in 1,000 games?
   A. Mike Marshall
   B. Kent Tekulve
   C. Hoyt Wilhelm
   D. Cy Young

4.16 Who was the first pitcher to win two Most Valuable Player awards?
   A. Bob Gibson
   B. Carl Hubbell
   C. Sandy Koufax
   D. Hal Newhouser

4.17 Three of these four players drove in 100 or more runs in each of 13 different seasons. Which one did not?
   A. Hank Aaron
   B. Jimmy Foxx
   C. Lou Gehrig
   D. Babe Ruth

4.18 What player had 300 or more total bases the most times in his career?
   A. Hank Aaron
   B. Lou Gehrig
   C. Pete Rose
   D. Babe Ruth

4.19 What player had 400 or more total bases the most times in his career?
   A. Hank Aaron
   B. Lou Gehrig
   C. Stan Musial
   D. Babe Ruth

4.20 Which of these players is *not* among the top three career leaders in total bases?
   A. Hank Aaron
   B. Willie Mays
   C. Stan Musial
   D. Babe Ruth

4.21 Who holds the career record for most home runs as a second baseman?
A. Charlie Gehringer
B. Joe Gordon
C. Rogers Hornsby
D. Joe Morgan

4.22 What switch-hitter was the first to hit home runs from both sides of the plate in the same game 10 different times?
A. Mickey Mantle
B. Eddie Murray
C. Reggie Smith
D. Roy White

4.23 Who has the record for the highest career batting average by a switch-hitter?
A. Frankie Frisch
B. Mickey Mantle
C. Pete Rose
D. Willie Wilson

4.24 Who holds the record for hitting the most career grand slams?
A. Yogi Berra
B. Lou Gehrig
C. Gil Hodges
D. Willie McCovey

4.25 Pete Rose broke Ty Cobb's career hits record when he got his 4,192nd hit in 1985. But whose record did Cobb break to become the all-time hits leader?
A. Cap Anson
B. Willie Keeler
C. Nap Lajoie
D. Honus Wagner

Answers and Explanations

4.1 **A. Hank Aaron** Aaron wound up with 3,771 hits.
Musial (Cardinals, 1941-63) stands fourth on the
all-time list with 3,630, and Speaker (Boston,
Cleveland, Washington, and Philadelphia, all of the
American League, 1907-28) is fifth with 3,515.
Yastrzemski (Boston, 1961-83) is currently either
sixth or seventh on the all-time list with 3,419,
according to the source used (see question 20.19 for
an explanation).

4.2 **B. runs** Each scored 2,174 runs—second only to Ty
Cobb's 2,245. Aaron leads Ruth in the other three
categories: 624 to 506 in doubles, 2,297 to 2,211 in
RBIs, and 6,856 to 5,793 in total bases. In both RBIs
and total bases, Aaron is the all-time leader; he ranks
eighth in doubles.

4.3 **D. Stan Musial** All 15 sluggers with more home runs
than Musial's 475 led the league at least once. In
1948, Musial missed by just one home run, when he
hit 39 (Ralph Kiner and Johnny Mize each had 40
that year).

4.4 **B. Lefty Grove** Grove's record of 300-141 (for the A's
and Red Sox, 1925-41) gave him a winning
percentage of .680. (Grove also had an outstanding
minor league record of 108-36, a percentage of .750,
in five seasons with the powerful Baltimore Orioles
of the International League.) Next best is Christy
Mathewson's .665 (373-187). Alexander's percentage
was .642 (373-208), Johnson's was .599 (416-279),
and Young's was .620 (511-313). The most recently
retired 300-game-winner to have a percentage above
.600 was Tom Seaver, with .603 (311-205).

4.5 **B Phil Niekro** Niekro won 318 and lost 274, a
percentage of .537, for the Braves, Yankees, Indians,
and Blue Jays, from 1964-87. Carlton's percentage

was .574 (329-244), Perry's was .542 (314-265), and Wynn's was .551 (300-244). Active 300-game-winner Nolan Ryan, though, will almost certainly finish his career with a percentage below Niekro's. At the end of the 1990 season, he was .526 (302–272).

4.6 **B. Cliff Johnson**   Playing for several teams (Houston, New York Yankees, Cleveland, Chicago Cubs, Oakland, Toronto, and Texas) from 1974-86, Johnson hit a total of 20. Next best is Jerry Lynch's 18, hit while playing for Cincinnati and Pittsburgh from 1957-66.

4.7 **D. Babe Ruth**   Ruth has the record, with 692 (686 in the American League and 6 in the National League), his other home runs coming as a pitcher and first baseman. As an outfielder, Aaron is second with 661; he hit his other homers as a first baseman, second baseman and designated hitter.

4.8 **A. Joe Morgan**   Morgan walked 1,799 times in the National League, from 1963-83, playing for Houston, Cincinnati, San Francisco, and Philadelphia (and 66 more times in the American League for Oakland in 1984). Musial had 1599, Ott had 1708, and Rose had 1566.

4.9 **B. Babe Ruth**   Ruth had 2,056. Williams is second with 2,019. Joe Morgan ranks third (1,865), Yastrzemski fourth (1,845), and Mantle fifth (1,734).

4.10 **B. 293**   This is the record since intentional walks began to be compiled in 1955. He had 289 in the National League and 4 in the American League.

4.11 **D. Ted Williams**   Williams's "walk average" was .208 (2,019 walks and 7,706 at-bats). Ruth had the second-best walk average, .197. If 4,000 at-bats is used as the minimum requirement, then Max Bishop, with 4,494 at-bats and a .204 walk average (playing

for the Philadelphia Athletics and Boston Red Sox
from 1924-35), ranks between Williams and Ruth.

4.12 **A. Hank Aaron**   Aaron had 1,477, consisting of 624
doubles, 98 triples, and 755 home runs. Of these long
hits, 1,429 were hit in the National League, which is
the National League record. Musial is second with
1,377, and Ruth is third with 1,356 (including a
record 1,350 in the American League).

4.13 **A. 121**   Hank Aaron holds the record. He hit 113 in the
National League and 8 in the American League. Don
Baylor holds the American League record of 115.

4.14 **B. Phil Niekro**   Young had 7,357, Galvin (playing from
1879-92 for Buffalo and for three different Pittsburgh
clubs in three different leagues), 5,941; Johnson,
5,926; and Niekro, 5,404.

4.15 **C. Hoyt Wilhelm**   Only Wilhelm and Tekulve have
ever done it. Wilhelm reached this plateau in 1970,
and ended up with 1,070 to Tekulve's 1,050. Lindy
McDaniel is third on the all-time games-pitched list,
with 987.

4.16 **B. Carl Hubbell**   Pitching for the Giants, Hubbell
won in 1933 and 1936. In 1933 he led the league in
wins (23, against 12 losses), ERA (1.66), innings
pitched (308.2) and shutouts (10). In 1936, he again
led the league in wins (26, against 6 losses) and
ERA (2.31), as well as won-lost percentage (.813).
Newhouser won the award twice in a row for
Detroit in 1944-45. Gibson (1968) and Koufax
(1963) each won the award once.

4.17 **A. Hank Aaron**   Aaron is not far behind the others,
though, having accomplished the feat 11 times.

4.18 **A. Hank Aaron**   Aaron did it 15 times. Gehrig has the
American League record of 13 times, all in
consecutive years (1926-38).

4.19 **B.** **Lou Gehrig**   Gehrig did it five times: 1927, 1930-31, 1934, and 1936. It is quite possible that this remarkable record will stand even longer than his record for playing in consecutive games.

4.20 **D.** **Babe Ruth**   Ruth's 5,856 total bases are only good enough for fifth on the all-time list behind Aaron (6,856), Musial (6,134), Mays (6,066), and Ty Cobb (5,856). Pete Rose ranks sixth, with 5,752.

4.21 **D.** **Joe Morgan**   Morgan hit 266, including 6 for Oakland in 1984. Rogers Hornsby holds the National League record with 263. Ryne Sandberg of the Chicago Cubs, whose 40 home runs in 1990 made him the first second baseman to lead the league in homers since Hornsby did it in 1925, could one day threaten these records.

4.22 **A.** **Mickey Mantle**   Mantle did it fot the tenth time in 1964. Eddie Murray equaled this total on June 9, 1990.

4.23 **A.** **Frankie Frisch**   Frisch's lifetime average, in a career from 1919-37 for the New York Giants and St. Louis Cardinals, was .316.

4.24 **B.** **Lou Gehrig**   Gehrig had 23. McCovey holds the National League record of 18. Others high on the list are Jimmy Foxx and Ted Williams with 17 each, Hank Aaron, Babe Ruth, and Dave Kingman with 16 each, Eddie Murray with 15, and Hodges with 14. Berra had 9.

4.25 **D.** **Honus Wagner**   Cobb passed him in 1923 (Wagner, who played in the National League for Louisville and Pittsburgh from 1897-1917, had retired with more than 3,400 hits.) The same year, Cobb also broke Wagner's lifetime record for runs scored (1,740).

Chapter 5

Leading the League

Unlike career records, single-season achievements can be set by most anyone. Players have been known to lead the league in a category for one season, then vanish into virtual obscurity. More often, though, a player who wins a batting title or leads the league in ERA isn't merely lucky—witness the number of repeat winners in the major statistical categories. One of the side benefits of having so many individual competitions to lead the league is that they add interest to the closing weeks of the season even when division races have already been decided. (Answers and explanations begin on page 52.)

    5.1 What pitcher led the National League in wins the most times during his career?
       A. Dizzy Dean
       B. Sandy Koufax
       C. Christy Mathewson
       D. Warren Spahn

    5.2 Who was the only rookie ever to win a batting title?
       A. Rod Carew
       B. Al Kaline
       C. Tony Oliva
       D. Lloyd Waner

5.3 What must a batter have in order to qualify for the batting title—apart from having the highest batting average?
A. 3.1 plate appearances for each game played by his team
B. 3.1 at-bats for each game played by his team
C. 500 plate appearances
D. 500 at-bats

5.4 What outfielder set a major league record by leading a league in assists seven times?
A. Roberto Clemente
B. Rocky Colavito
C. Joe DiMaggio
D. Carl Yastrzemski

5.5 Who was the last American League player to win the Triple Crown?
A. Don Mattingly
B. Jim Rice
C. Frank Robinson
D. Carl Yastrzemski

5.6 Who was the last National League player to win the Triple Crown?
A. Rogers Hornsby
B. Chuck Klein
C. Joe Medwick
D. Frank Robinson

5.7 Which of these players never won a Triple Crown?
A. Lou Gehrig
B. Mickey Mantle
C. Willie Mays
D. Ted Williams

5.8 Which of these players *did* win a Triple Crown?
A. Hank Aaron
B. Jimmy Foxx
C. Stan Musial
D. Babe Ruth

5.9 The "pitcher's Triple Crown" is an informally recognized achievement that consists of leading the league in all but which of these pitching statistics?
A. ERA
B. strikeouts
C. wins
D. won-lost percentage

5.10 Which of these pitchers won the "pitcher's Triple Crown" more than once?
A. Steve Carlton
B. Bob Feller
C. Sandy Koufax
D. Tom Seaver

5.11 Three players share the record of leading the American League in total bases six times. Who is *not* one of them?
A. Ty Cobb
B. Jimmy Foxx
C. Babe Ruth
D. Ted Williams

5.12 Who has won the most National League home run crowns?
A. Hank Aaron
B. Ralph Kiner
C. Willie Mays
D. Mike Schmidt

5.13 Three of these pitchers won 300 games without ever leading his league in victories. Which of these 300-game winners *did* lead his league in wins at least once?
A. Gaylord Perry
B. Eddie Plank
C. Nolan Ryan
D. Don Sutton

5.14 In which offensive category did sportscaster and former catcher Tim McCarver once lead the National League?
A. singles
B. doubles
C. triples
D. home runs

5.15 What pitcher led the National League in strikeouts a record seven consecutive times?
  A. Christy Mathewson
  B. Tom Seaver
  C. Warren Spahn
  D. Dazzy Vance

5.16 How many batting titles did Rod Carew win?
  A. 1
  B. 4
  C. 7
  D. 10

5.17 Who was the first White Sox player to win a batting title?
  A. Luke Appling
  B. Eddie Collins
  C. Joe Jackson
  D. Minnie Minoso

5.18 Who holds the record for leading a league (or tying for the league lead) in home runs the most consecutive times?
  A. Hank Aaron
  B. Ralph Kiner
  C. Babe Ruth
  D. Ted Williams

5.19 What pitcher holds the record for leading the league in walks the most times?
  A. Bob Feller
  B. Sam McDowell
  C. Nolan Ryan
  D. Bob Turley

5.20 Three National Leaguers share the record for leading the league in RBIs the most times—four times each. Who is *not* one of them?
  A. Hank Aaron
  B. Rogers Hornsby
  C. Johnny Mize
  D. Mike Schmidt

5.21 Who holds the record for leading a league in singles the most consecutive years?
   A. Richie Ashburn
   B. Wade Boggs
   C. Nellie Fox
   D. Pete Rose

5.22 What pitcher holds the record for leading a league in ERA the most times?
   A. Grover Cleveland Alexander
   B. Lefty Grove
   C. Sandy Koufax
   D. Christy Mathewson

5.23 Who was the first player since 1900 to have a season batting average at least 50 points higher than any other player in either league?
   A. George Brett
   B. Rod Carew
   C. Ty Cobb
   D. Ted Williams

5.24 Which of these events has *never* happened in American League history?
   A. A catcher wins a batting title.
   B. A player who wins a batting title has his average drop more than 100 points the following year.
   C. A player hits over .400 but fails to win the batting title.
   D. The winner of the batting title is at least 40 years old.

5.25 Which of these events *has* happened in National League history?
   A. A catcher wins a batting title.
   B. A player who wins a batting title has his average drop more than 100 points the following year.
   C. A player hits over .400 but fails to win the batting title.
   D. The winner of the batting title is at least 40 years old.

Answers and Explanations

5.1 **D. Warren Spahn**   Spahn did it an amazing eight
times, all for the Braves: (1949, 1950, 1953,
1957-61). Walter Johnson has the American League
record, six times (1913-16, 1918, 1924).

5.2 **C. Tony Oliva**   Oliva led the American League with a
.323 batting average for Minnesota in 1964. As a
rookie for Pittsburgh in 1927, Waner hit .355, but he
finished third behind his brother Paul (who was also
his teammate), who hit .380, and Rogers Hornsby,
who hit .361 for New York.

5.3 **A. 3.1 plate appearances for each game played by his
team**   A batter can also win the title if he is short of
the required number of plate appearances—
provided that if he were to go 0-for-whatever
number of at-bats are needed to bring him up to the
minimum number of required plate appearances, he
would still win the title. This last nuance was added
in 1967 (although a similar rule had been in effect
from 1951-55, when the minimum at-bats total was
400). The 3.1 at-bats-per-game formula was
instituted in 1957.

5.4 **D. Carl Yastrzemski**   Yastrzemski did it for Boston in
1962-64, 1966, 1967, 1971, and 1977. Clemente
holds the National League record of five league leads
in assists, having done it for Pittsburgh in 1958,
1960-61, and 1966-67.

5.5 **D. Carl Yastrzemski**   In 1967, Yastrzemski led the
league with a .326 average, 44 home runs, and 121
RBIs.

5.6 **C. Joe Medwick**   Playing for St. Louis in 1937,
Medwick batted .374 with 31 home runs (this tied
him for the league lead with Mel Ott, but his Triple
Crown is no less valid), and 154 RBIs. Hornsby

(Cardinals) won the Triple Crown twice, in 1922 (.401, 42, 152) and 1925 (.403, 39, 143), and Klein (Phillies) won it in 1933 (.368, 28, 120). Robinson had some great National League seasons, but won his one Triple Crown in the American League in 1966, playing for Baltimore (.316, 49 home runs, 122 RBIs).

5.7 **C. Willie Mays** Gehrig did it in 1934 with a .363 batting average, 49 home runs, and 165 RBIs. Mantle did it in 1956 (.353, 52, 130). Williams did it twice—just before and after his years in the armed services during World War II. In 1942, he hit .356 with 36 home runs and 137 RBIs; and in 1946, he hit .343 with 32 home runs and 114 RBIs. Mays led the league in batting once (.345 in 1954) and in home runs four times (1955, 1962, 1964-65), but even though he's seventh on the all-time RBI list, Mays never led the league in RBIs.

5.8 **B. Jimmy Foxx** Foxx won it in 1933 (.356, 48, 163). Aaron just missed in 1963, when he led the league in home runs (44, tied with Willie McCovey) and RBI (130), but finished third in batting, just seven points below Tommy Davis of Los Angeles (and one point behind Pittsburgh's Roberto Clemente). In 1948, Musial hit 39, one less than Pittsburgh's Ralph Kiner or New York's Johnny Mize. With one more homer that year, Musial could have won the "Septuple Crown," if there were such a thing, as he led the league in batting (.376), hits (230), doubles (46), triples (18), runs (135), and RBIs (131). Ruth narrowly missed a Triple Crown twice: In 1924, he led the league in batting (.378) and home runs (46), but his 121 RBIs were 8 short of the 129 hit by Washington's Goose Goslin; and in 1926, he led the league in home runs (47) and RBIs (145), but his .372 average was six points less than that of Heinie Manush of Detroit.

5.9 **D. won-lost percentage** To a team, won-lost percentage might seem to be more important than

wins or strikeouts. On the other hand, the hitters'
Triple Crown is not made up of the statistics that best
measure a player's value: Both slugging average and
on-base average, for example, are probably better
indicators of a hitter's performance than batting
average (and if you multiply SA and OBA together,
you get an even more accurate measure by which to
compare players).

5.10 **C. Sandy Koufax**   Pitching for Los Angeles, Koufax
did it three times: 1963 (25 wins, 1.88 ERA, 306
strikeouts), 1965 (26, 2.04, 382), and in his final
season, 1966 (27, 1.73, 317). Carlton led the league
in all three categories for Philadelphia in 1972 (27,
1.97, 310). Seaver led the league in wins three times,
in ERA three times, and in strikeouts five times—but
he never led in all three categories at once. Feller led
the league in wins six times and in strikeouts seven
times, but never led in ERA.
　　　Koufax's triple Triple is amazing, but not unique:
Pitching for Washington, Walter Johnson led the
league in all three categories in 1913 (36, 1.09, 243),
1918 (23, 1.27, 162) and 1924 (23, 2.72, 158). And
Grover Cleveland Alexander did it *four* times (three
times for the Phillies, once for the Cubs): 1915 (31,
1.22, 241), 1916 (33, 1.55, 167), 1917 (30, 1.86,
201), and 1920 (27, 1.91, 173).

5.11 **B. Jimmy Foxx**   Cobb led the league in total bases in
1907, 1908, 1909, 1911, 1915, and 1917; Ruth in
1919, 1921, 1923, 1924, 1926, 1928; Williams in
1939, 1942, 1946, 1947, 1949, and 1951. Hank
Aaron holds the National League (and major league)
record of leading the league eight times: in 1956,
1957, 1959, 1960, 1961, 1963, 1967, and 1969.

5.12 **D. Mike Schmidt**   Schmidt won eight (1974-76, 1980,
1981, 1983, 1984, 1986). Kiner led the league in
home runs seven times, while Aaron and Mays each
did it four times. Babe Ruth has the American League
record, having led the league 12 times (see question
5.18).

5.13 **A. Gaylord Perry**   Perry, who won 314 games from 1962 to 1983, led the National League with 23 wins for San Francisco in 1970, and again for San Diego with 21 wins in 1978. He also led the American League with 24 wins for Cleveland in 1972.

Plank won 327 games from 1902-12 for Philadelphia and St. Louis of the American League, and St. Louis of the Federal League. He was a 20-game winner seven times—with as many as 26 wins in a season—but he never led the league in wins. Ryan, who won his 300th game in 1990, had his greatest number of wins in 1974 (22 for California), but Catfish Hunter (Oakland) and Ferguson Jenkins (Texas) each won 25 that year. Sutton won 324 games, playing for several different teams from 1966-88, but only once won 20 games. That year (1976), his 21 wins left him one win short of Randy Jones, who won 22 for San Diego. Plank, Ryan, and Sutton are the only three pitchers to reach the 300-win plateau without leading their league in victories at least once. Bert Blyleven, who is closing in on 300 wins, could become the fourth pitcher to achieve this distinction.

5.14 **C. triples**   He hit 13 triples in 1966 for the St. Louis Cardinals. He is, in fact, the only National League catcher ever to lead the league in triples. (In the American League, though, Carlton Fisk of Boston had 9 triples in 1972 to tie Oakland's Joe Rudi for the league lead.)

5.15 **D. Dazzy Vance**   Pitching for Brooklyn, Vance led the league from 1922-28. His high was 262 strikeouts in 1924. Walter Johnson did even better in the American League, leading in strikeouts eight consecutive years (1912-19).

5.16 **C. 7**   He won batting titles in 1969, 1972-75, 1977, and 1978. This ties him for third on the all-time batting crown list behind Ty Cobb (12 titles) and Honus Wagner (8). (The other seven-time winners were Stan Musial and Rogers Hornsby.) Carew also had 15 straight years over .300 (1969-83)—only Cobb, Musial, and Wagner had more consecutive .300 seasons.

5.17 **A. Luke Appling** Appling, who played his entire career for the White Sox from 1930-50, led the league with a .388 average in 1936 (as well as with a .328 average in 1943). Lifetime, Collins had a higher batting average for the White Sox (.331, from 1915-26) than Appling (.310), but never won a batting title. Jackson had the highest lifetime average (.340) of any member of the White Sox, but had the misfortune of playing during some of Ty Cobb's best years. Minoso hit .304 lifetime for the White Sox (1951-57, 1960-61, 1964, 1976, 1980), but never led the league.

5.18 **B. Ralph Kiner** Kiner did it from 1946-52 (tying in 1947-48). Ruth's best streak was six consecutive home run crowns, 1926-31 (tying in 1931), but had he not missed large numbers of games in 1922 (when he played in 110 games, hitting 35 home runs) and in 1925 (when he hit 25 home runs in 98 games), he would probably have led the league 14 years in a row, since he did so every other year from 1918-31.

5.19 **C. Nolan Ryan** Ryan did it eight times: six in the American League, playing for California (1972-74, 1976-78) and twice in the National League, playing for Houston (1980, 1982). Six of those times, though, he also led the league in strikeouts, with his strikeouts always far exceeding his walks (usually by about a 2-to-1 ratio). Pitching for Cleveland, Feller led the league in walks four times in six years (1938-46), and McDowell did it five times in six years (1965-70), but neither did it any other time. Turley led the league three times, for Baltimore in 1954 and the Yankees in 1955 and 1958.

5.20 **C. Johnny Mize** Mize came close, though, with league-leading seasons in 1940 for the Cardinals, and

1942 and 1947 for the Giants. Aaron led in 1957, then
every third year for awhile (1960, 1963, 1966).
Hornsby led while playing for St. Louis in 1920-22
and 1925. Schmidt, for Philadelphia, led in 1980-81,
1984, and 1986.

5.21 **C. Nellie Fox**   Fox did it seven years in a row, playing
for the White Sox from 1954-60. He also led the
league in singles in 1952, giving him eight singles
titles in all—also a major league record.

5.22 **B. Lefty Grove**   Pitching for Philadelphia and Boston,
Grove led the American League nine times: 1926,
1929-32, 1935-36, and 1938-39. Alexander, Koufax,
and Mathewson led the National League in ERA a
record five times each. Alexander (Philadelphia and
Chicago) did it first in 1915, last in 1920; Koufax
(Los Angeles) did it consecutively from 1962-66; and
Mathewson (New York) did it first in 1905 and last in
1913.

5.23 **B. Rod Carew**   Playing for Minnesota in 1977, Carew
hit .388. The next best average in baseball that year
was Dave Parker's .338 for Pittsburgh. The
second-place finisher in the American League was
Carew's teammate Lyman Bostock, who hit .336.

5.24 **A. A catcher wins a batting title.**   No American
League catcher has ever led the league in hitting.
After winning the batting title, Norm Cash (Detroit)
dropped a record 118 points, from .361 in 1961 to
.243 in 1962. Joe Jackson (Cleveland) hit .408 in
1911, but was second to Ty Cobb's .420. Ted
Williams won the batting title at age 40 in 1958.

5.25 **A. A catcher wins a batting title.**   Two catchers
achieved this: Bubbles Hargrave for Cincinnati in
1926, and Ernie Lombardi, both for Cincinnati in
1938 and Boston in 1942. National Leaguers came
close to the other feats, though. Willie McGee won
the batting title with a .353 average for St. Louis in
1985, then dropped 99 points, to .254, the following

year. In 1930 Babe Herman hit .393 for Brooklyn, but finished second to Bill Terry's .401. Honus Wagner is the oldest National League batting crown winner, leading the league at age 37 in 1911.

Chapter 6

All the Bases

It's time to take a break from the last two chapters' statistical tests. Like Chapter 1, this quiz touches all the bases, but you may find it a little bit harder. (Answers and explanations begin on page 65.)

6.1 How many balls do umpires typically prepare—by rubbing them with mud to remove the factory gloss—for a single game?
   A. one dozen
   B. three dozen
   C. five dozen
   D. seven dozen

6.2 In which two years were there players' strikes that shortened the season?
   A. 1969 and 1978
   B. 1972 and 1981
   C. 1975 and 1984
   D. 1978 and 1987

6.3 Which of these stadiums has artificial turf?
   A. Fenway Park in Boston
   B. Memorial Stadium in Baltimore
   C. Milwaukee County Stadium
   D. Royals Stadium in Kansas City

6.4 Who unsuccessfully challenged baseball's reserve clause when his team tried to trade him in 1969, charging that baseball was in violation of antitrust laws and taking the case all the way to the Supreme Court?
   A. Curt Flood
   B. Catfish Hunter
   C. Ferguson Jenkins
   D. Joe Morgan

6.5 Who is the all-time leader in career singles?
   A. Ty Cobb
   B. Pete Rose
   C. Tris Speaker
   D. Honus Wagner

6.6 How has the percentage of games completed by starting pitchers changed since 1900?
   A. It has decreased from 85 percent to 11 percent.
   B. It has decreased from 65 percent to 21 percent.
   C. It has decreased from 45 percent to 31 percent.
   D. It has increased from 25 percent to 30 percent.

6.7 In the last 50 years, how has the average number of innings pitched by starting pitchers changed?
   A. It has gone from 8 to 4.
   B. It has gone from 8 to 5.
   C. It has gone from 7 to 5.
   D. It has gone from 7 to 6.

6.8 Which of these team feats has been achieved more than once in the twentieth century?
   A. Two players on a team each hit at least 50 home runs in the same season.
   B. Three players on a team each hit at least 40 home runs in the same season.
   C. Four players on a team each hit at least 30 home runs in the same season.
   D. Six players on a team each hit at least 20 home runs in the same season.

6.9 In 1990, Jose Canseco raised his fee for a personal appearance on the autograph-signing circuit to $50,000, making
him the highest-priced guest-for-hire among both present
and former major leaguers. Until Canseco raised his fee,
what former major leaguer charged the most money per appearance?
   A. Hank Aaron
   B. Joe DiMaggio
   C. Mickey Mantle
   D. Willie Mays

6.10 American League president (and former Yankee player)
Dr. Bobby Brown is what kind of doctor?
   A. cardiologist
   B. dentist
   C. optometrist
   D. psychologist

6.11 What is the most strikeouts by both teams combined in a
single extra-inning game?
   A. 23
   B. 33
   C. 43
   D. 53

6.12 How far from the batter's circle are the on-deck circles?
   A. 17 feet
   B. 27 feet
   C. 37 feet
   D. 47 feet

6.13 What team, at various times in its history, was known as
the Red Stockings, Doves, and Beaneaters?
   A. Braves
   B. Reds
   C. Red Sox
   D. White Sox

6.14 When was the first Negro National League founded?
   A. 1880
   B. 1900
   C. 1920
   D. 1940

6.15 Which formula will give you a team's magic number for winning a division?
  A. Add 1 to the number of games ahead the team is in the loss column from its closest opponent, then subtract the result from the number of games the team has left to play.
  B. Add 1 to the number of games the team has left to play, and subtract the number of games ahead the team is in the loss column from its closest opponent.
  C. Add the team's wins to its closest opponent's losses, subtract the result from 162, and divide by two; if the result is a fraction, round it up.
  D. Take the number of games ahead the team is in the standings, double it, and subtract the number of additional games, if any, that the team has played in comparison to its closest opponent.

6.16 Which of these sluggers had the highest lifetime batting average?
  A. Hank Aaron
  B. Mickey Mantle
  C. Willie Mays
  D. Frank Robinson

6.17 Who holds the career record for most home runs as as catcher?
  A. Johnny Bench
  B. Yogi Berra
  C. Gary Carter
  D. Carlton Fisk

6.18 In this century, what is the greatest number of games out of first place that a team has finished a season?
  A. 22 1/2 games
  B. 44 1/2 games
  C. 66 1/2 games
  D. 88 1/2 games

6.19 What player with more than 350 career home runs struck out fewer than 400 times?
- **A.** Yogi Berra
- **B.** Joe DiMaggio
- **C.** Stan Musial
- **D.** Mel Ott

6.20 If the number of times a player led a league in batting, home runs, and RBIs are added together, what player has the highest total?
- **A.** Ty Cobb
- **B.** Rogers Hornsby
- **C.** Babe Ruth
- **D.** Ted Williams

6.21 What team appeared in the most League Championship Series during the 1980s?
- **A.** Kansas City
- **B.** Los Angeles
- **C.** Oakland
- **D.** St. Louis

6.22 Each of these players played at first base for more than 1,000 games, and also at some other position for more than 1,000 games ("outfield" counting as one position). Which one played more games at first than any of the others?
- **A.** Ernie Banks
- **B.** Rod Carew
- **C.** Ron Fairly
- **D.** Stan Musial

6.23 Who was the first National League pitcher this century to strike out 200 or more batters in each of his first two major league seasons?
- **A.** Dwight Gooden
- **B.** Carl Hubbell
- **C.** Tom Seaver
- **D.** Dazzy Vance

6.24 Of players active in 1990, who was the career leader in RBIs at the end of that season?
A. George Brett
B. Eddie Murray
C. Dave Parker
D. Dave Winfield

6.25 As of 1990, what franchise fee was the National League planning to charge a city that is chosen as the home of a new team when the league expands in 1993?
A. $95,000
B. $950,000
C. $9,500,000
D. $95,000,000

Answers and Explanations

6.1 **C. five dozen**   For a doubleheader, they prepare eight dozen. The umpire takes three to start, keeping two in his pockets. The gloss is removed by rubbing the balls with Lena Blackburne's Baseball Rubbing Mud, which comes from the banks of the Delaware River. Blackburne (whose real first name was Russell) was a utility player 1910–19, managed the White Sox in 1928-29, and appeared in one game as a pitcher in 1929. He began marketing the mud after finding that it removes the gloss without discoloring the balls.

6.2 **B. 1972 and 1981**   In 1972, a strike at the beginning of the season was quickly settled, with only a 6–9 games lost from the schedule. In 1981, however, a 50-day midseason strike resulted in the drawing up of special "split-season" rules to cover postseason play. In each of baseball's four divisions, the team with the best record in the first part of the season played a best-of-five playoff against the team with the best record in the second part of the season. Serious inequities resulted, however; St. Louis, for example, did not make the playoffs despite having the best record in the National League East over the entire season.

6.3 **D. Royals Stadium in Kansas City**   It is the only one of the league's 11 nondomed stadiums without a natural surface. Artificial turf is more common in the National League, where it can be found in six of 12 parks.

6.4 **A. Curt Flood**   Arthur Goldberg, the former Supreme Court justice, represented Flood in the case. Baseball won the suit, but the reserve clause was eventually modified to allow free agency.

6.5 **B. Pete Rose**   Rose hit 3,215. Cobb, with 3,052, holds the American League record.

6.6　**A.　It has decreased from 85 percent to 11 percent.**
By 1960, it had decreased by nearly two-thirds to
around 30 percent; since then, it has again dropped by
about two-thirds.

6.7　**D.　It has gone from 7 to 6.**　This might seem
surprising, in view of the answer to the previous
question, but the change is not as small as it looks.
Also, even though far fewer starters finish a game
these days than in 1940, they still tend to stay in the
game (on their good days) until the eighth inning or
so before a manager is likely to call on a late-inning
relief specialist.

6.8　**D.　Six players on a team each hit at least 20 home
runs in the same season.**　This has actually
happened four times: The New York Yankees did it in
1961, the Minnesota Twins in 1964, the Milwaukee
Braves in 1965, and the Detroit Tigers in 1986, each
had six players who hit 20 or more home runs. The
other three feats happened only once each. The 1961
Yankees had two players with 50 home
runs—Mickey Mantle (54) and Roger Maris (61).
The 1973 Atlanta Braves had three players with 40—
Hank Aaron (40), Darrell Evans (41), and Davey
Johnson (43). And the 1977 Dodgers had four players
with 30—Dusty Baker (30), Ron Cey (30), Steve
Garvey (33), and Reggie Smith (32).

6.9　**B.　Joe DiMaggio**　In 1990, DiMaggio's fee was
$45,000, and the next highest was Mantle's fee of
$40,000. It is remarkable that Canseco, in only his
fifth full year in the majors, was able to market
himself more successfully than such Hall of Fame
players.

6.10　**A.　cardiologist**　He is an M.D., a licensed cardiologist,
and a graduate of Tulane Medical School. Brown, as
a part-time third baseman, hit .279 for the Yankees
from 1946-54, and had a .439 batting average (18 for
41) in 17 World Series games in 1947 and 1949-51.

6.11 **C. 43** California vs. Oakland, July 9, 1971, in 20 innings. California batters struck out 26 times (also a record) and Oakland batters struck out 17 times.

6.12 **C. 37 feet** Each on-deck circle is five feet in diameter.

6.13 **A. Braves** Originally called the Boston Red Stockings, the team became known as the Beaneaters late in the nineteenth century. The name "Doves" was briefly used when George Dovey was the team president. The name Braves came into use in 1912, when Tammany Hall chieftain Jim Gaffney owned the club. And during the latter half of the 1930s, the club was known as the Bees.

6.14 **C. 1920** Begun by Andrew (Rube) Foster, the league lasted until 1931. By then, other leagues for black players had sprung up; the last such league, the Negro American League, lasted until 1960, 13 years after Jackie Robinson had become the first black player on a modern major league team. The Negro Leagues, as they are collectively known, typically played a short schedule of league games, but the teams would play additional games against various black or white independent clubs. Some Negro League stars, such as Satchel Paige, later played in the majors. In 1971, a Special Committee on the Negro Leagues began to consider Hall of Fame membership of Negro League players, and several have since been inducted into the Hall.

6.15 **B. Add 1 to the number of games the team has left to play, and subtract the number of games ahead the team is in the loss column from its closest opponent.** The magic number is the total of team wins and/or opponent's losses that are needed for the team to clinch its division.

6.16 **A. Hank Aaron** Aaron hit .305; Mantle, .298; Mays, .302; and Robinson, .294.

6.17 **D. Carlton Fisk** Fisk tied Bench's record of 327 home runs as a catcher on August 8, 1990, and hit his 328th on August 17 to break the record.

6.18   **C.   66 1/2 games**   In 1906, Boston, with a record of 49-102, finished 66 1/2 games behind the National League-leading Cubs, who were 116-36. The American League record for distant finishes was set by the St. Louis Browns in 1939, when their 43-111 record left them 64 1/2 games behind the Yankees (106-45). (In 1899, Cleveland finished 84 games behind Brooklyn in the National League.)

6.19   **B.   Joe DiMaggio**   DiMaggio had 361 home runs and only 369 strikeouts—a remarkable ratio for a power hitter. Babe Ruth, for example, struck out nearly twice as often as he homered, and Mike Schmidt struck out more than three times for every home run. Berra also had an exceptionally good ratio, with 358 home runs and just 415 strikeouts. Musial had 475 home runs and 696 strikeouts, and Ott had 511 home runs and 896 strikeouts. There are other exceptions, but most players with 350 or more home runs have well over 1,000 strikeouts.

6.20   **C.   Babe Ruth**   Ruth led in Triple Crown departments 19 times: once in batting, 12 times in home runs, and 6 times in RBIs. Cobb had the next best total (17), leading the league in batting 12 times, home runs once, and RBIs 4 times. Williams is third (16) with a very balanced 6 batting titles, 6 home run crowns, and 4 RBI titles. Hornsby is fourth (15), having led the league in batting 7 times, home runs twice, and RBIs 4 times.

6.21   **B.   Los Angeles**   Los Angeles appeared in four, in 1981, 1983, 1985, and 1988. The other three choices were tied for second, with three LCS appearances each: Kansas City in 1980 and 1984-85, Oakland in 1981 and 1988-89, and St. Louis in 1982, 1985, and 1987.

6.22   **A.   Ernie Banks**   Banks played 1,259 games at first, as well as 1,125 at shortstop (all for the Chicago Cubs,

1953-71). Banks, Carew (with 1,184 games played at first and 1,130 at second), Fairly (1,218 at first, 1,037 in the outfield), and Musial (1,016 at first, 1,886 in the outfield) are the only four players in history to have played at least 1,000 games at each of two positions. (Since "outfield" is considered one position in this question, Babe Ruth's 1,054 games in leftfield and 1,133 in rightfield count as 2,187 games played in one position.)

6.23   **A.   Dwight Gooden**   Both of Gooden's totals, 276 in 1984 and 268 in 1985, were also good enough to lead the league. Hubbell's highest season strikeout total was 159 in 1937, the only year in which he led the league. Seaver had 170 strikeouts in 1967, his rookie year, before reeling off a major league record nine consecutive seasons of more than 200. Vance led the league in strikeouts in each of his first full six seasons, but did so with totals of only 134 and 197 his first two years.

6.24   **D.   Dave Winfield**   Winfield was first, reaching 1,500 in late 1990 and ending in the season with 1,516. Parker was second (1,434), followed closely by Brett (1,398) and Murray (1,373).

6.25   **D. $95,000,000**   It cost $100,000 just to apply. The nearly $100,000,000 fee was so high, and dollars in many cities so tight, that a number of prospective cities dropped out of the running in 1990. The league, though, was trying to make things easier by allowing cities to pay on an installment basis.

Chapter 7

Heavy Hitters

There's little doubt that most fans love to see a lot of hitting when they go to the ballpark—preferably by the team they're rooting for. Low-scoring games can be exciting and well-played...but having lots of players running around the bases is downright fun.

A hitter has only a fraction of a second in which to decide whether to swing at a pitch, and to figure out whether the ball will be high or low, inside or outside, straight or breaking. Hitting tests the limits of human beings' vision, reflexes, and dexterity; and for some major leaguers, the results are amazing. (Answers and explanations begin on page 75.)

7.1 Who was the first twentieth century player to get at least 200 hits in each of seven consecutive years?
A. Wade Boggs
B. Rod Carew
C. Ty Cobb
D. Rogers Hornsby

7.2 Which of these batting feats has been accomplished by the *fewest* players?
A. batting in 2,000 runs
B. scoring 2,000 runs
C. striking out 2,000 times
D. walking 2,000 times

7.3 Which of these batting feats has been accomplished by the most players?
   A. a career slugging average of over .600 (based on at least 4,000 total bases)
   B. 600 or more career doubles
   C. 600 or more career home runs
   D. 600 or more career stolen bases

7.4 Who holds the National League record for most home runs in a season?
   A. Hank Aaron
   B. Ralph Kiner
   C. Willie Mays
   D. Hack Wilson

7.5 Who holds the major league record for most total bases in a season?
   A. Lou Gehrig
   B. Rogers Hornsby
   C. Stan Musial
   D. Babe Ruth

7.6 Who was the last player to have 400 or more total bases in a season?
   A. Hank Aaron
   B. Jose Canseco
   C. Roger Maris
   D. Jim Rice

7.7 Who was the last player to have a slugging average of .700 or more for a single season?
   A. Joe DiMaggio
   B. Dave Parker
   C. Mike Schmidt
   D. Ted Williams

7.8 Who holds the major league record for hitting 30 or more home runs the most consecutive seasons?
   A. Hank Aaron
   B. Jimmy Foxx
   C. Eddie Mathews
   D. Babe Ruth

7.9 In all the seasons in which Bobby Bonds hit more than 30 home runs, for how many different teams did he play?
   A. 1
   B. 3
   C. 5
   D. 7

7.10 Who holds the season record for most home runs by a player who was at least 40 years old at the end of the season?
   A. Hank Aaron
   B. Darrell Evans
   C. Jim Rice
   D. Ted Williams

7.11 Ty Cobb and who are the only two players to hit at least one home run both as a teenager and after their 40th birthday?
   A. Darrell Evans
   B. Al Kaline
   C. Brooks Robinson
   D. Rusty Staub

7.12 Who was the first black player to collect 3,000 hits?
   A. Hank Aaron
   B. Ernie Banks
   C. Lou Brock
   D. Willie Mays

7.13 Who walked five times in a game on four different occasions—the only person to have more than two five-walk games?
   A. Mickey Mantle
   B. Mel Ott
   C. Babe Ruth
   D. Ted Williams

7.14 Who holds the record for the most RBIs in a season?
   A. Jimmy Foxx
   B. Lou Gehrig
   C. Babe Ruth
   D. Hack Wilson

7.15 Who holds the record for the most extra-base hits in a season?
A. Hank Aaron
B. Lou Gehrig
C. Babe Ruth
D. Ted Williams

7.16 Who holds the record for hitting two or more home runs in a game the most times?
A. Hank Aaron
B. Hank Greenberg
C. Willie Mays
D. Babe Ruth

7.17 Who hit three or more home runs in a game the most times?
A. Jimmy Foxx
B. Johnny Mize
C. Babe Ruth
D. Mike Schmidt

7.18 Three of these players hit four consecutive home runs in a single game. Which one did not?
A. Rocky Colavito
B. Lou Gehrig
C. Babe Ruth
D. Mike Schmidt

7.19 In what year did Joe DiMaggio have his record 56-consecutive-game hitting streak?
A. 1936
B. 1941
C. 1946
D. 1951

7.20 Who hit more home runs than anyone else during the 1950s?
A. Gil Hodges
B. Mickey Mantle
C. Stan Musial
D. Duke Snider

7.21 Who hit more home runs than anyone else during the 1970s?
A. Reggie Jackson
B. Dave Kingman
C. Mike Schmidt
D. Willie Stargell

7.22 Who has the record for the highest season batting average by a switch hitter in this century?
A. Frankie Frisch
B. Mickey Mantle
C. Pete Rose
D. Willie Wilson

7.23 Who hit the most grand slams in a single season?
A. Ernie Banks
B. Lou Gehrig
C. Jim Gentile
D. Don Mattingly

7.24 Who had the most home runs going into an All-Star Game—not counting years in which there were two All-Star Games?
A. Reggie Jackson
B. Dave Kingman
C. Roger Maris
D. Willie McCovey

7.25 In 1935, American League All-Star competition for first base was especially tough. Jimmy Foxx was heading toward a home run crown, hitting a round-tripper once every 6.7 at-bats, to go with a .346 batting average; Lou Gehrig would go on to hit .329 and to lead the league in runs and walks, and finish second in RBIs; and Hank Greenberg already had 100 RBIs after just 75 games, and wound up with 170 for the season, along with a .328 batting average. So who played first base for the American League All-Stars that year?
A. Jimmy Foxx
B. Lou Gehrig
C. Hank Greenberg
D. all of them, playing three innings each

Answers and Explanations

7.1 **A. Wade Boggs** Boggs did it from 1983-89. His streak was broken in 1990, when he collected 187 hits. He was also the first to do it six consecutive years. (Willie Keeler did it eight straight years, from 1894–1901, on a shorter schedlue.)

7.2 **C. striking out 2,000 times** Only Reggie Jackson, with 2,597 strikeouts, has accomplished this "feat." Two players, Hank Aaron and Babe Ruth, had over 2,000 RBIs; two, Ruth and Ted Williams, had over 2,000 walks; and five, Aaron, Ty Cobb, Willie Mays, Pete Rose, and Ruth, scored more than 2,000 runs.

7.3 **D. 600 or more career stolen bases** Four players have slugging averages over .600. Nine players have at least 600 doubles (Tris Speaker has the most with 793, followed by Pete Rose, Stan Musial, Ty Cobb, Nap Lajoie, John Wagner, Carl Yastrzemski, Hank Aaron, and Paul Waner); three have at least 600 home runs (Hank Aaron, Babe Ruth, and Willie Mays); and 18 have at least 600 stolen bases (Willie Wilson of Kansas City and Tim Raines of Montreal were the last to reach this mark, in 1990).

7.4 **D. Hack Wilson** Wilson, then age 30, hit 56 for Chicago in 1930. He had hit 30 or more home runs three times previously, but in 1931 slumped to just 13. By age 34, his major league career was over, and his career home run total of 244 now lies far down the all-time list.

7.5 **D. Babe Ruth** Ruth collected 457 for the New York Yankees in 1921. Hornsby holds the National League record with 450 for St. Louis in 1922.

7.6 **D. Jim Rice** For Boston in 1978, Rice had 406, consisting of 127 singles, 25 doubles, 15 triples, and 46 home runs.

7.7　**D.　Ted Williams**　Williams slugged a torrid .731 for
　　　　Boston in 1957. Musial was the last to do it in the
　　　　National League, with a .702 mark in 1948.

7.8　**B.　Jimmy Foxx**　Foxx, playing in the American League
　　　　for Philadelphia and Boston, did it for 12 straight
　　　　seasons (1929-40). Mathews holds the National
　　　　League record of 9, set playing for Milwaukee from
　　　　1953-61.

7.9　**C.　5**　The teams, and the years in which he hit over 30
　　　　home runs, were San Francisco in 1969, 1971, and
　　　　1973, the New York Yankees in 1975, California in
　　　　1977, and the Chicago White Sox and Texas in 1978.

7.10　**B.　Darrell Evans**　Evans, who turned 40 in May 1987,
　　　　hit 34 home runs for Detroit that year. Aaron set the
　　　　National League record of 20 home runs by a
　　　　40-year-old in 1974.

7.11　**D.　Rusty Staub**　Staub hit six home runs for Houston
　　　　as a 19-year-old rookie in 1963. He hit his last home
　　　　run in 1985, at age 41, playing for the Mets. During
　　　　his 23-year career, he hit 292 home runs in all,
　　　　including a high of 30 for Montreal in 1970. Cobb
　　　　actually hit a home run at age 18, another one at 19
　　　　(for Detroit in 1905-06), as well as five at 40 and one
　　　　at 41 (for the A's in 1927–28).

7.12　**D.　Willie Mays**　Mays reached the 3,000 mark in 1970,
　　　　and ended up with 3,283. Aaron wound up with
　　　　3,771, Banks with 2,583, and Brock with 3,023.

7.13　**B.　Mel Ott**　Ott did it in 1929, 1933, 1943, and
　　　　1944—helped, no doubt, by the fact that he was only
　　　　5'-9", making him the shortest player ever to hit 500
　　　　home runs in his career. The overall record for walks
　　　　in a modern, nine-inning game, though, is six by
　　　　Jimmy Foxx, who did it playing for Boston on June
　　　　16, 1938. Walter Wilmot of the Cubs walked six
　　　　times on August 22, 1891; and Andre Thornton of

Cleveland walked six times in a 16-inning game on May 2, 1984.

7.14 **D. Hack Wilson**   Wilson drove in 190 runs for the Chicago Cubs in the heavy–hitting season of 1930, which sported a league batting average of .303! It was the same year in which his home run record was set (see question 7.4). No one in either league has even threatened his single-season RBI record in many decades. Wilson also led the league in RBIs the year before, with an impressive total of 159.

7.15 **C. Babe Ruth**   Ruth had 119 "long hits" in 1921 (44 doubles, 16 triples, and 59 home runs).

7.16 **D. Babe Ruth**   Ruth did it 72 times (71 times in the American League and once in the National League). Mays holds the National League record, having hit two or more home runs in 63 games. The single-season mark belongs to Greenberg, who did it 11 times in 1938 for Detroit.

7.17 **B. Johnny Mize**   Mize did it six times. He did it for the Cardinals twice in 1938 and twice in 1940, and once each for the Giants (1947) and Yankees (1950). Dave Kingman is in second place, having hit three home runs in a game on five occasions, 1976, 1978, 1979 twice, and 1984.

7.18 **C. Babe Ruth**   The first to do so in the twentieth century was Lou Gehrig on June 3, 1932 for the Yankees. Ruth never hit four home runs in a game, consecutive or otherwise. Other players have hit four home runs in a game, but only Colavito, Gehrig, and Schmidt have done it in consecutive trips to the plate.

7.19 **B. 1941**   From May 15 to July 16. During the streak, he was 91-for-223, a .406 batting average. The modern National League record batting streak is 44 by Pete Rose in 1978 for Cincinnati.

7.20 **D. Duke Snider**   Snider hit 326 home runs from

1950-59. Of the four years (1954-57) that Snider and the crosstown centerfielders Mickey Mantle and Willie Mays all played together in New York, Snider led the other two in total home runs and RBIs. Hodges was second in the decade with 310, followed by Mathews (299), Mantle (280), Stan Musial (266), Yogi Berra (266), and Mays (250).

7.21 **D. Willie Stargell**   Stargell hit 296 home runs from 1970-79. Next best during the decade were Jackson (292), Johnny Bench (290), Bobby Bonds (280), Lee May (270), Kingman (252), and Graig Nettles (also 252). Schmidt was further back with just 235 home runs in the 1970s, but was the leader in the 1980s with 313, edging Dale Murphy's 308.

7.22 **B. Mickey Mantle**   Mantle's .365 average in 1956 is the best in this century. In the National League, the modern record is Willie McGee's .353 mark for the Cardinals in 1985, although George Davis hit .355 for the Giants in 1893. The best all-time is Tommy Tucker's .372 with Baltimore in the American Association in 1889.

7.23 **D. Don Mattingly**   Mattingly hit six for the New York Yankees in 1987. Gentile hit five in 1961 for Baltimore, and Banks hit five for the Cubs in 1955 (the National League single-season record).

7.24 **A. Reggie Jackson**   Playing for Oakland in 1969, Jackson had already hit 37 after 92 games. For the rest of the season, however, he hit just 10 more, and he finished third in the league behind Harmon Killebrew (Minnesota), who hit 49, and Frank Howard (Washington), who hit 48.

7.25 **B. Lou Gehrig**   Gehrig played the entire game at first base, and Foxx, chosen as the alternate first baseman, played the entire game at third (and drove in three runs). Greenberg did not even make the team(!), but did have the considerable consolation of winning the Most Valuable Player award for the pennant-winning Tigers that year.

Chapter 8

Masters of the Mound

Some have claimed that pitching is 90 percent of the game. That's an exaggeration, surely, but the edge pitchers hold over batters is apparent from the fact that no batter in history has a lifetime on–base percentage of .500 (Ted Williams holds the record, a .483 mark).

When a pitcher is "on," it almost does not seem to matter who the hitters are—as when Carl Hubbell struck out five future Hall of Famers (Babe Ruth, Lou Gehrig, Jimmy Foxx, Al Simmons, and Joe Cronin) in succession, in the 1934 All-Star Game. This quiz is devoted to baseball's much-heralded, hard-working hurlers. (Answers and explanations begin on page 85.)

8.1 What pitcher most often had the honor of being the starting pitcher on his team's opening game of the season?
A. Steve Carlton
B. Walter Johnson
C. Tom Seaver
D. Warren Spahn

8.2 What is the twentieth century record for most wins in a season by a single pitcher?
  A. 26
  B. 31
  C. 36
  D. 41

8.3 What 300-game winner had fewer than 200 wins at age 40?
  A. Phil Niekro
  B. Gaylord Perry
  C. Don Sutton
  D. Early Wynn

8.4 The Giants' Rick Reuschel has been called the game's most "action-oriented" pitcher, because a higher percentage of the balls he throws are batted into play than balls thrown by any other pitcher. On average, what percentage of major league pitches—by all pitchers—are batted into play?
  A. 1 out of 3
  B. 1 out of 4
  C. 1 out of 5
  D. 1 out of 6

8.5 When Ron Guidry tied an American League record for a lefthanded pitcher with nine shutouts in 1978, whose record did he tie?
  A. Whitey Ford
  B. Lefty Grove
  C. Eddie Plank
  D. Babe Ruth

8.6 Who set a record by being the first to strike out 20 batters in a nine-inning game?
  A. Steve Carlton
  B. Roger Clemens
  C. Bob Feller
  D. Nolan Ryan

8.7 What pitcher set a record by being the first to strike out 10 consecutive batters in a game?
A. Sandy Koufax
B. Jim Maloney
C. Nolan Ryan
D. Tom Seaver

8.8 Who was the first pitcher after Cy Young to win over 100 games and strike out more than 1,000 batters *in each league*?
A. Jim Bunning
B. Gaylord Perry
C. Nolan Ryan
D. Don Sutton

8.9 Who set a record in 1990 for the most saves in a season?
A. Dennis Eckersley
B. John Franco
C. Dave Righetti
D. Bobby Thigpen

8.10 Don Sutton's match-up against Phil Niekro on June 28, 1986, was the first between 300-game winners since what year?
A. 1892
B. 1922
C. 1952
D. 1982

8.11 What pitcher set a modern record for winning the highest percentage of games won by his team in a single season?
A. Steve Carlton
B. Lefty Grove
C. Nolan Ryan
D. Tom Seaver

8.12 What is the most consecutive wins a pitcher has ever had without a loss (ignoring no-decision games)?
A. 14
B. 19
C. 24
D. 29

8.13 How old was Satchel Paige when he made his last major league appearance?
A. 44
B. 49
C. 54
D. 59

8.14 Who holds the record for winning the most games in relief?
A. Rollie Fingers
B. Sparky Lyle
C. Kent Tekulve
D. Hoyt Wilhelm

8.15 Nolan Ryan is the all-time major league career strikeout leader, with over 5,000. Who is second on the list?
A. Steve Carlton
B. Walter Johnson
C. Tom Seaver
D. Cy Young

8.16 Of these four pitchers, who threw the most career shutouts?
A. Don Drysdale
B. Bob Feller
C. Sandy Koufax
D. Juan Marichal

8.17 Of these four pitchers, who threw the most career shutouts?
A. Bob Gibson
B. Jim Palmer
C. Tom Seaver
D. Don Sutton

8.18 How many pitchers have won 300 or more games in their careers, including nineteenth-century hurlers?
A. 10
B. 20
C. 40
D. 80

8.19 Who once gave up only 21 walks in 306 innings—the lowest single-season walk-per-inning ratio in this century for a pitcher with at least 300 innings pitched?
A. Walter Johnson
B. Sandy Koufax
C. Christy Mathewson
D. Cy Young

8.20 Who pitched the only modern eight-inning complete game no-hitter—losing 4-0?
A. Steve Barber
B. Andy Hawkins
C. Ken Johnson
D. Jim Maloney

8.21 How many major league games did Babe Ruth win as a pitcher?
A. 14
B. 54
C. 94
D. 134

8.22 Who had three one-hitters in four consecutive starts at the end of 1988 and beginning of 1989?
A. Roger Clemens
B. Mike Scott
C. Dave Stieb
D. Frank Viola

8.23 What pitcher had the most wins during the 1960s?
A. Jim Bunning
B. Sandy Koufax
C. Bob Gibson
D. Juan Marichal

8.24 What pitcher had the most wins during the 1970s?
A. Steve Carlton
B. Ferguson Jenkins
C. Jim Palmer
D. Tom Seaver

8.25 What pitcher had the most wins during the 1980s?
  A. Jack Morris
  B. Nolan Ryan
  C. Dave Stieb
  D. Fernando Valenzuela

Answers and Explanations

8.1 **C. Tom Seaver**   Seaver opened 16 seasons: 13 in the
National League (for New York and Cincinnati,
during the period 1967-83) and 3 in the American
League (for Chicago, 1984-86).

8.2 **D. 41**   Jack Chesbro won 41 games for New York
(American League) in 1904, while also setting a
modern single-season record of 48 complete games.
The National League record is held by Christy
Mathewson, with 37 wins for the New York Giants in
1908.

8.3 **A. Phil Niekro**   Phil Niekro had only 197 wins then,
and had had only 31 on his 30th birthday. He ended
up with a career record of 318-274.

8.4 **C. 1 out of 5**   A more exact figure is 21 percent.
Reuschel's average, though, is 1 out of 3.

8.5 **D. Babe Ruth**   Ruth pitched 9 shutouts for Boston in
1916. The National League record is 11, set by Sandy
Koufax for the Dodgers in 1963. For righthanders,
the record is Grover Cleveland Alexander's 16 for the
Phillies in 1916 (which matched the pre-twentieth
century record of 16 set by George Bradley, pitching
for St. Louis in 1876).

8.6 **B. Roger Clemens**   Clemens did it for Boston against
Seattle on April 30, 1986, as part of a season in which
he won both the Most Valuable Player and Cy Young
awards.

8.7 **D. Tom Seaver**   Pitching for the New York Mets,
Seaver struck out 10 consecutive San Diego Padres
on April 22, 1970.

8.8 **A. Jim Bunning**   Bunning, who was elected to
Congress from Kentucky in 1986, also pitched a

no-hitter in each league, one a perfect game. When he
retired, his career strikeout total of 2,885 was second
only to Walter Johnson's. His lifetime record was
224-184, with an ERA of 3.27, playing for Detroit,
Philadelphia, Pittsburgh, and Los Angeles from
1955-71.

8.9 **D. Bobby Thigpen**   On September 2, with a month still
left in the season, Thigpen of the Chicago White Sox
broke the old record of 46, set by Righetti in 1986 for
the New York Yankees. Thigpen ended up with a total
of 57 saves for the season, and Dennis Eckersley of
Oakland was second with 48.

8.10 **A. 1892**   The opposing 300-game winners that year
were Tim Keefe of Philadelphia and Pud Galvin of
Pittsburgh and St. Louis.

8.11 **A. Steve Carlton**   Carlton won 27 games (against just
10 losses) for Philadelphia in 1972, the most wins
ever for a pitcher on a last-place team—and his wins
amounted to 45.8% of the team's wins. Overall, the
Phillies were 59-97 that year, a .378 winning
percentage; without Carlton's decisions, they would
have been 32-87, a .269 percentage.

8.12 **C. 24**   Carl Hubbell of the New York Giants won 24 in
a row in 1936-37. The American League record is 17,
shared by Dave McNally (Baltimore, 1968-69) and
Johnny Allen (Cleveland, 1936-37).

8.13 **D. 59**   Twelve years after his previous major league
appearance, which had been for the St. Louis Browns
in 1953, he pitched three shutout innings for Kansas
City against Boston on September 25, 1965, giving
up only one hit to Carl Yastrzemski. That made Paige
the oldest ever to play in a major league game.

8.14 **D. Hoyt Wilhelm**   Wilhelm won 123 games (and lost
102) as a relief pitcher from 1952-72, playing for the
Giants, Cardinals, Indians, Orioles, White Sox,
Angels, Braves, Cubs, and Dodgers. Used

occasionally as a starter, (he pitched a no-hit game over the Yankees), he had an overall won-lost record of 143-122, with 227 saves.

8.15 **A. Steve Carlton**   Carlton is second with 4,136, which is also the record for a lefthanded pitcher. Seaver is third (3,640), followed by Don Sutton, Bert Blyleven, Gaylord Perry, and Johnson.

8.16 **D. Juan Marichal**   Marichal had 52. The others' totals are: Drysdale, 49; Feller, 46; and Koufax, 40.

8.17 **C. Tom Seaver**   Seaver had 61; Sutton, 58; Gibson, 56; and Palmer, 53.

8.18 **B. 20**   Nolan Ryan became the twentieth to do it when he defeated the Milwaukee Brewers on July 31, 1990.

8.19 **C. Christy Mathewson**   Mathewson did it in 1913, pitching for the New York Giants; he averaged giving up one walk every 14.6 innings. The following year, he had nearly as good a ratio, with just 23 walks in 312 innings pitched. Young, pitching for Boston in 1904, set the American League record, with 29 walks in 380 innings (one walk every 13.1 innings). With fewer than 300 innings pitched, Babe Adams had a slightly better ratio than Mathewson. Pitching for Pittsburgh in 1920, Adams gave up only 18 walks in 263 innings (1 walk per 14.61 innings; Mathewson's ratio works out to 14.57).

8.20 **B. Andy Hawkins**   On June 30, 1990, Hawkins (of the Yankees) lost to Chicago because of four unearned runs in the eighth inning. One player reached on an error and stole second. Then after two walks, a two-out fly was dropped by rookie leftfielder Jim Leyfritz, allowing three runs to score. Finally, Jesse Barfield in rightfield dropped another fly ball (apparently lost in the sun)—the Yankees' third error of the inning—adding another run.

   The other pitchers listed as choices also had some bad luck in no-hit games. Johnson lost a nine-inning

no-hitter 1-0 in 1964, pitching for Houston against
Cincinnati. Maloney pitched 10 innings of no-hit ball
for Cincinnati against New York in 1965, losing 1-0
on two hits in the 11th. And Harvey Haddix pitched
12 perfect innings in 1959 for Pittsburgh against
Milwaukee, before giving up a hit in the 13th and
losing 1-0 on an unearned run.

8.21   **C.   94**   His lifetime record was 94-46—a superb
winning percentage of .671—and he was also 3-0 in
World Series competition. He was 89-46 for Boston,
5-0 for the Yankees. He was a 20-game winner in
1916 and 1917, and he won 18 in 1915.

8.22   **C.   Dave Stieb**   Pitching for Toronto, Stieb became the
first ever to do it. Perhaps the only comparable
low-hit feat is Johnny Vander Meer's two consecutive
no-hitters, which he threw for Cincinnati against
Boston and Brooklyn on June 11 and June 15, 1938.
Stieb has been known for many dramatic low-hit
games: Prior to throwing his first career no-hitter in
1990, he had on four different occasions pitched a
no-hitter through eight complete innings, only to
have someone get a hit in the ninth.

8.23   **D.   Juan Marichal**   Marichal had 191. Gibson was
second with 164, followed by Don Drysdale (158),
Bunning (150), and Jim Kaat (142). Koufax only
pitched through 1966, but still had 137.

8.24   **C.   Jim Palmer**   Palmer won 186 games from 1970-79.
Gaylord Perry was second with 184 wins, followed
by Carlton, Jenkins, and Seaver with 178 each.

8.25   **A.   Jack Morris**   Morris won 162. Stieb was second
with 143, followed by Bob Welch (137), Valenzuela
(128), Bert Blyleven (123), and Ryan (122).

Chapter 9

By Any Other Name

Baseball fields have always been fertile ground for the creation of nicknames. Sometimes a new name is born practically overnight, as when Frank "Home Run" Baker got his nickname as a result of hitting home runs on successive days against Rube Marquard and Christy Mathewson of the Giants in the 1911 World Series, and not from leading the league in home runs (though he did that, too). Other times, a nickname goes back to a player's childhood. Team names, too, have often changed, being subject to changing times, reflecting the preference of a new owner or a catchy name that a sportswriter first coined. Here, then is a baseball "name game." (Answers and explanations begin on page 94.)

9.1 What player, who batted a record .650 in a League Championship Series in 1989, is nicknamed "The Natural"?
   A. George Bell
   B. Will Clark
   C. Carney Lansford
   D. Ryne Sandberg

9.2 Who gave pitcher Jim Hunter the nickname "Catfish"?
   A. his club's owner
   B. his father
   C. a sportswriter
   D. his wife

9.3 What was the original name of the Boston Red Sox?
    A. Puritans
    B. Red Stockings
    C. Somersets
    D. Whalers

9.4 What team was originally known as the Blues, then Bronchos, and later the Naps after Nap Lajoie joined them in 1902?
    A. Cleveland Indians
    B. Chicago White Sox
    C. Philadelphia Athletics
    D. Philadelphia Phillies

9.5 Who was the first player to have a candy bar named after him?
    A. Reggie Jackson
    B. Candy Maldonado
    C. Kid Nichols
    D. Babe Ruth

9.6 What was Whitey Ford's nickname?
    A. "Chairman of the Board"
    B. "The Kentucky Colonel"
    C. "The Old Professor"
    D. "The Silver Fox"

9.7 Whose nickname is, or was, "The Wizard of Oz"?
    A. Claude Osteen
    B. Ozzie Smith
    C. Ozzie Virgil (Jr.)
    D. Ozzie Virgil (Sr.)

9.8 How did "Pee Wee" Reese get his nickname?
    A. He didn't—he was born with the name Pee Wee.
    B. His Dodger teammates gave him the name because he was the shortest player on the team.
    C. He used to shoot marbles a lot, and a "pee wee" is a kind of marble.
    D. A sportswriter gave him the name while he was in the minor leagues because Reese reminded him of a cartoon character named Pee Wee.

9.9 How did Commissioner Kenesaw Mountain Landis get his name?
   A. His real name was Ken; but as a five-year old child, after a camping trip with his parents, he kept repeating "Kenny saw a mountain."
   B. He was named for a Civil War battle.
   C. He was named for a place in a popular novel.
   D. He was named for the place he was born.

9.10 What player, nicknamed "Senator," won an All-Star starting spot by means of write-in votes in 1974?
   A. Cesar Cedeno
   B. Darrell Evans
   C. Steve Garvey
   D. Bill Madlock

9.11 Whose bat was nicknamed "Black Betsy"?
   A. Ty Cobb
   B. Rogers Hornsby
   C. Joe Jackson
   D. Babe Ruth

9.12 Who were known as "Big Poison" and "Little Poison"?
   A. Felipe and Matty Alou
   B. Dizzy and Paul Dean
   C. Bob and Roy Johnson
   D. Paul and Lloyd Waner

9.13 Who was known as "The Mechanical Man"?
   A. Charlie Gehringer
   B. Bill Mazeroski
   C. Walter Johnson
   D. Vic Raschi

9.14 Who were the original "Hitless Wonders"?
   A. the 1906 Chicago White Stockings
   B. the 1932 Chicago Cubs
   C. the 1944 St. Louis Browns
   D. the 1969 New York Mets

9.15 Who was known as "Smiling Stan"?
  A. Stan Hack
  B. Stan Musial
  C. Stan Williams
  D. Eddie Stanky

9.16 Who was known as "The Beast"?
  A. Orlando Cepeda
  B. Jimmie Foxx
  C. Frankie Frisch
  D. Willie McCovey

9.17 Who was born with a string of names beginning "Saturnino Orestes Arrieta Armas"?
  A. Tony Armas
  B. Juan Marichal
  C. Minnie Minoso
  D. Tony Oliva

9.18 Which Hall of Famer was named after another Hall of Famer?
  A. Whitey Ford
  B. Lefty Gomez
  C. Mickey Mantle
  D. Willie McCovey

9.19 Collectively, teammates Frank "Home Run" Baker, Stuffy McInnis, Eddie Collins, and Jack Barry had what nickname?
  A. "The $100,000 Infield"
  B. "The Gas House Gang"
  C. "The Hitless Wonders"
  D. "Murderers' Row"

9.20 Who was known as "The Flying Dutchman"?
  A. Dutch Leonard (Hubert Benjamin)
  B. Dutch Leonard (Emil John)
  C. Johnny Vander Meer
  D. Honus Wagner

9.21 Which was *not* the nickname of one of the DiMaggio brothers?
A. "Goofy"
B. "Joltin' Joe"
C. "The Yankee Clipper"
D. "The Little Professor"

9.22 What is Bert Blyleven's full name?
A. Albert van Blyleven
B. Betrand Russell Blyleven
C. Richard Burton Blyleven
D. Rik Aalbert Blyleven

9.23 What was Johnny Mize's nickname?
A. "The Big Cat"
B. "The Georgia Peach"
C. "The Splendid Splinter"
D. "The Toy Cannon"

9.24 When they began playing in New York in 1903, what was the name of the team that is now the New York Yankees?
A. New York Bombers
B. New York Highlanders
C. New York Metropolitans
D. New York Yankees

9.25 What American Association player, the namesake of a twentieth century politician, hit .435 in 1887 for St. Louis?
A. Bill Bradley
B. Gerald Ford
C. Dick Nixon
D. Tip O'Neill

Answers and Explanations

9.1 **B. Will Clark** Clark, San Francisco's star first
baseman, is also nicknamed "Will the Thrill." He was
also the first player to sign a contract that would earn
him $4 million in a future season.

9.2 **A. his club's owner** A's owner Charles O. Finley did it
to create media interest in Hunter. Various stories
were spread about how he had acquired the name
while a North Carolina farm boy, but they were
apocryphal.

9.3 **A. Puritans** Also known as the Pilgrims, the team
briefly changed its name to the Somersets (when their
owner was Charlie Somers), then became the Red
Sox soon after John Taylor bought them in the 1910s.

9.4 **A. Cleveland Indians** Lajoie, the sixth player elected
to the Hall of Fame, jumped from the Phillies to the
A's in 1901. The Phillies sued to keep him from
playing in Pennsylvania, and league president Ban
Johnson avoided potential legal problems by sending
Lajoie to Cleveland, where he played from 1902-14
before returning to the A's.

9.5 **A. Reggie Jackson** Reggie Bars were showered on
spectators at Yankee Stadium each time Jackson
would hit a home run. Although many people think
Baby Ruth candy bars were named for Babe Ruth,
they were actually named for Grover Cleveland's
young daughter Ruth, who was often seen playing on
the White House lawn while he was in office.

9.6 **A. "Chairman of the Board"** "The Kentucky
Colonel" was Earle Combs, who hit well over .300
nine times and was the leadoff hitter on the powerful
late-'20s Yankee teams. "The Old Professor" was
Casey Stengel, who managed the Yankees to 10

pennants, and "The Silver Fox" was Brooklyn
Dodger slugger and centerfielder Duke Snider.

9.7 **B. Ozzie Smith**   Smith earned the name because of his
defensive wizardry at shortstop. He is considered by
many to be the best defensive player ever at that
position. After starting his career with San Diego in
1978, he was traded to St. Louis after the 1981
season. An All-Star and Gold Glove winner nearly
every year in the '80s, he has set numerous shortstop
records, such as most assists in a season (621 in
1980).

9.8 **C. He used to shoot marbles a lot, and "pee wee" is a
kind of marble.**   Harold Henry Reese, who at 5'10"
was not at all short, was a champion marble shooter.
He was also known as the "Little Colonel," because
he once played for the Louisville Colonels of the
American Association.

9.9 **B. He was named for a Civil War battle.**   Landis was
named for the June, 1864, Civil war battle of
Kennesaw Mountain in Georgia where his father was
wounded. (His first name was spelled with one "N,"
however.) He is best known for taking a hard line on
corruption within the game. He banned the eight
bribery-implicated Chicago "Black Sox" players for
life, and several more players—and even owners—at
other times. Prior to his tenure as commissioner
(1920-44), he had served as an Illinois federal district
court judge, where he heard an antitrust suit brought
by the newly formed Federal League against the
National and American Leagues. He delayed his
decision until the Federal League had collapsed, and
grateful owners remembered him when, during the
tumultuous aftermath of the Black Sox scandal, they
needed to pick a strong commissioner.

9.10 **C. Steve Garvey**   The nickname referred to Garvey's
political ambitions. Garvey, a lifetime .294 hitter,
played for Los Angeles from 1969-82 and for San
Diego from 1983-87. He set a National League record

by playing in 1,207 consecutive games, and set a
major league record for fielding percentage at first
base for a season (1.000, in 1984). In 1974, the year
he made the All-Star team by write-in, he ended up
winning the Most Valuable Player awards for both the
All-Star Game and his season's play. His numbers
that year included 200 hits, a .312 average, 21 home
runs, and 111 RBIs.

9.11 **C. Joe Jackson**   And Jackson could certainly hit with
it: After Cobb's .367 and Hornsby's .358, Jackson's
lifetime average of .356 is third on the all-time
batting list.

9.12 **D. Paul and Lloyd Waner**   Both playing for
Pittsburgh, the Waners had 460 hits between them in
1927—an all-time record for brothers that seems
unlikely to be broken, considering how few players
ever reach half that hit total in a season. Paul's 237
hits led the league that year, and Lloyd was second
with 223.

9.13 **A. Charlie Gehringer**   Gehringer was a consistent
hitter (lifetime .320) and an excellent-fielding second
baseman who played his entire career for Detroit
(1924-42). Mazeroski, a top-flight second baseman
for Pittsburgh who played from 1956-72, had no
special nickname other than "Maz"; 1907-27
Washington pitching ace Johnson was known as "The
Big Train" or "Barney"; Raschi, a star Yankee pitcher
from 1946-53 (who finished his career with the
Cardinals and Kansas City), was "The Springfield
Rifle."

9.14 **A. the 1906 Chicago White Stockings**   Chicago won
the American League pennant despite a team batting
average of .230 (the lowest ever for a pennant
winner) and a club total of just six home runs
throughout the entire year, then upset the highly
favored Cubs, four games to two, in the only
all-Chicago World Series in history. The White
Stockings, however, did have quite a pitching staff.

Led by Frank Owen (22-13), Nick Altrock (20-13), Doc White (18-6), and Ed Walsh (17-13), their staff had a season ERA of a minuscule 2.13 (though one team in the league did even better—Cleveland, with an ERA of 2.09).

9.15 **A. Stan Hack**   Hack was a lifetime .301 hitter in 16 seasons (1932-47) for the Cubs, for whom he usually played third base. In 18 World Series games (1932, 1935, 1938, and 1945), he hit .348 (24 for 69). Musial was known as "Stan the Man"; Stanky, who played in the National League for Chicago, Brooklyn, Boston, New York, and St. Louis from 1943-53, was "The Brat" or "Muggsy"; Williams, who pitched for Los Angeles, the New York Yankees, Cleveland, Minnesota, St. Louis, and Boston from 1958-72, had no particular nickname.

9.16 **B. Jimmy Foxx**   Foxx, who had a powerful body build, played most of his career with the Athletics and Red Sox and was one of the most feared power hitters ever. He hit 58 home runs in 1932 and is fourth on the all-time slugging average list. His other nickname was "Double X."

Cepeda was known as "The Baby Bull" because his father was known as both "The Bull" and the "Babe Ruth of Puerto Rico." Frisch was "The Fordham Flash," and McCovey's nickname was "Stretch."

9.17 **C. Minnie Minoso**   Born Saturnino Orestes Arrieta Armas Minoso, the lifetime .298 hitter had many remarkable accomplishments during his career, but none so unusual as playing in five different decades. He began his career in 1949 with Cleveland, but had his best years with the White Sox. Although his career had seemingly ended in 1964, the White Sox activated him for three games in 1976 (he had one hit that year, making him, at 53, the oldest player ever to get one), then used him twice in 1980 as a pinch-hitter. In 1990, plans were under consideration to activate him again at age 68, which would have

made him the first six-decade player, until
Commissioner Fay Vincent vetoed the idea as being a
publicity stunt that would hurt the integrity of the
game. The only other five-decade player was Nick
Altrock, who pitched from 1898 to 1909 for several
clubs and then served for many years as a
Washington coach and clown who made occasional
appearances in official games up to 1933.

9.18 **C. Mickey Mantle**   Mantle was named after his
father's favorite player, Mickey Cochrane. Cochrane,
who played for the Athletics and Tigers from
1925-37, was a two-time Most Valuable Player (1928
and 1934), and has the highest lifetime batting
average of any major league catcher (.320). From
1934-38, while still a player, he was also a successful
manager for Detroit, with World Series appearances
in 1934-35.

9.19 **A. "The $100,000 Infield"**   Connie Mack assembled
the topnotch infield, which played for the
Philadelphia Athletics from 1911-14. He broke them
up, rather than pay the high salaries necessary to keep
players from jumping to the rival Federal League.
"The Gas House Gang" refers to the St. Louis
Cardinals teams of the 1930s, epitomized by such
characters as pitcher Dizzy Dean and third
baseman/outfielder Pepper Martin. "Murderers'
Row" refers to the top Yankee teams of the late
1920s, including the 1927 team that had highest
slugging percentage in history (.489) and included
the league's top three players in total bases that year
(Babe Ruth, Lou Gehrig, and Earle Combs), as well
as the dangerous Tony Lazzeri. The 1927 Yankee
team finished with a record of 110-44, and may have
been the best team ever. Besides their awesome
lineup, they had the league's top two pitchers in ERA
and won-lost percentage, Waite Hoyt (2.63, .759) and
Urban Shocker (2.84, .750).

9.20 **D. Honus Wagner**   One of the first five players elected
to the Hall of Fame, Wagner hit .329 in 21 seasons for

Louisville and Pittsburgh (1897-1917), setting many offensive career records that have since been broken. He was the first player to have his signature on a bat (a 1905 Louisville Slugger), and his picture is on the most valuable baseball card (see question 11.19).

The two Dutch Leonards, by the way, were both pitchers: Emil was 191-181 for Brooklyn, Washington, the Phillies, and the Cubs from 1933-53, and Hubert, often called "Hub," was 139-112 for the Red Sox and Detroit from 1913-1925. Vander Meer's nicknames were "The Dutch Master" and "Double No-Hit," the latter referring to his unique feat of tossing two consecutive no-hitters in 1938.

9.21 **A.** **"Goofy"**   "Goofy" was the nickname of Lefty Gomez. Joe DiMaggio was, of course, known as both "Joltin' Joe" and "The Yankee Clipper." His brother Dom was "The Little Professor," while his brother Vince had no particular nickname.

9.22 **D.** **Rik Aalbert Blyleven**   He was born in the Netherlands, in the town of Zeist. Although arm trouble threatened his career in late 1990, at the time he had more wins than any active pitcher except Nolan Ryan, with chances to reach 300.

9.23 **A.** **"The Big Cat"**   Mize, an outstanding hitter for both power and average during his career (1936-42, 1946-53), was both large and "graceful as a cat." "The Georgia Peach" was Ty Cobb, "The Splendid Splinter" was Ted Williams (who was also known as "The Thumper"), and "The Toy Cannon" was Jimmy Wynn (who played from 1963-77 for Houston, Los Angeles, Atlanta, the Yankees, and Milwaukee).

9.24 **B.** **New York Highlanders**   Established as the Baltimore Orioles when the American League began play in 1901, the team moved to New York in 1903, becoming the Highlanders (because they played in Upper Manhattan's Hilltop Park). Jim Price of the *New York Press* is credited with originating the name "Yankees," and it was officially adopted in 1913. The

Metropolitans was a New York American Association
club, whose name was shortened for use by the Mets.

9.25 **D. Tip O'Neill**   James "Tip" O'Neill, from Woodstock,
      Ontario, was Canada's greatest hitter in the majors.
      Although bases on balls were included as hits in
      1887, O'Neill's currently listed batting average of
      .435 is based only on his 225 hits and does not
      include his 50 walks. He also led the American
      Association in doubles, triples, and home runs, a rare
      feat indeed.

Chapter 10

The Rest of the Records

Hitting and pitching records are the most visible categories of baseball records, but fielding, baserunning, and service records have been keys to getting more than one player into the Hall of Fame. And let's not forget the managers, who, while (usually) not playing on the field, seem to have the most at stake (i.e., their jobs) when a team is playing poorly. (Answers and explanations begin on page 106.)

10.1 Lou Gehrig's streak of playing in 2,130 consecutive games is one of the best known records in baseball. But who has the second-longest streak?
A. Ty Cobb
B. Steve Garvey
C. Cal Ripken Jr.
D. Pete Rose

10.2 Who pitched in the majors the most seasons?
A. Tommy John
B. Phil Niekro
C. Warren Spahn
D. Cy Young

10.3 What player has the record for being a member of the
      "30-30" club—consisting of players with at least 30
      home runs and 30 stolen bases in a season—the most
      times in his career?
      A. Bobby Bonds
      B. Jose Canseco
      C. Howard Johnson
      D. Willie Mays

10.4 Joe McCarthy was the first manager to win pennants in
      both leagues. Who was the second?
      A. Sparky Anderson
      B. Yogi Berra
      C. Miller Huggins
      D. Casey Stengel

10.5 Rusty Staub is the only player to collect more than 500
      hits for each of four teams. Which was *not* one of these
      teams?
      A. Detroit
      B. Houston
      C. Montreal
      D. Texas

10.6 Pete Rose is the only player to have played 500 or more
      games at each of four different positions (counting
      "outfield" as a single position). At which of these
      positions did he play the *fewest* games?
      A. first base
      B. second base
      C. third base
      D. outfield

10.7 In 1988-89, Vince Coleman of the St. Louis Cardinals set
      a record for the for the most consecutive steals without
      being caught. How many?
      A. 10
      B. 30
      C. 50
      D. 70

10.8 What shortstop set lifetime records for games, double plays, and assists—and also led the American League for nine straight years in stolen bases?
- **A.** Luis Aparicio
- **B.** Cal Ripken Jr.
- **C.** Phil Rizzuto
- **D.** Everett Scott

10.9 What manager won a record seven All-Star Games?
- **A.** Walt Alston
- **B.** Sparky Anderson
- **C.** Billy Martin
- **D.** Casey Stengel

10.10 When Carl Yastrzemski played his 23rd year with the Boston Red Sox, whose record did he tie for playing the most seasons with a single club?
- **A.** Al Kaline
- **B.** Stan Musial
- **C.** Mel Ott
- **D.** Brooks Robinson

10.11 With how many different teams did manager Dick Williams win a pennant?
- **A.** 1
- **B.** 2
- **C.** 3
- **D.** 4

10.12 Who holds the National League record for the most games caught?
- **A.** Johnny Bench
- **B.** Roy Campanella
- **C.** Gary Carter
- **D.** Joe Garagiola

10.13 Who holds the career record for the most lifetime steals of home?
- **A.** Luis Aparicio
- **B.** Lou Brock
- **C.** Ty Cobb
- **D.** Maury Wills

10.14 What outfielder set a record for most consecutive chances handled without an error?
  A. Paul Blair
  B. Curt Flood
  C. Cesar Geronimo
  D. Terry Puhl

10.15 Who set a record in 1990 by playing 95 consecutive games at shortstop without making an error?
  A. Kevin Elster
  B. Spike Owens
  C. Cal Ripken Jr.
  D. Ozzie Smith

10.16 From the hiring of Bill Virdon on January 3, 1974, through the hiring of Carl (Stump) Merrill on June 6, 1990, inclusive, how many times did the New York Yankees change managers?
  A. 6
  B. 12
  C. 18
  D. 24

10.17 What pitcher holds the fielding record for being involved in the most double plays?
  A. Freddie Fitzsimmons
  B. Bob Lemon
  C. Phil Niekro
  D. Warren Spahn

10.18 How many outfielders have been involved in 100 or more double plays during their careers?
  A. 2
  B. 8
  C. 22
  D. 88

10.19 Which of these major league players managed in the major leagues for the most seasons?
  A. Cap Anson
  B. Lou Boudreau
  C. Joe Cronin
  D. Leo Durocher

10.20 Which of these former players *never* managed in the major leagues?
A. Ty Cobb
B. Stan Musial
C. Mel Ott
D. Cy Young

10.21 Who made the most putouts in the World Series as a first baseman?
A. Lou Gehrig
B. Gil Hodges
C. Wally Pipp
D. Moose Skowron

10.22 Who holds the career record for making the most putouts in All-Star Games?
A. Yogi Berra
B. Lou Gehrig
C. Willie Mays
D. Brooks Robinson

10.23 For which position is the individual record for consecutive games played without an error the highest?
A. catcher
B. first base
C. outfield
D. pitcher

10.24 For which position is the individual record for consecutive games played without an error the *lowest?*
A. catcher
B. second base
C. shortstop
D. third base

10.25 For which position is the individual record best fielding percentage for a season, based on 100 or more games, the *lowest*?
A. catcher
B. second base
C. third base
D. shortstop

Answers and Explanations

10.1 C. Cal Ripken Jr. On June 30, 1990, at age 29, Ripken
tied Everett Scott's second-place record of 1,307
consecutive games, and broke it two days later. As
this book goes to print, Ripken is still in a position to
break Gehrig's mark—though to do so, he will have
to play until the middle of the 1995 season without
missing a game. In all the games in Ripken's streak,
incidentally, Ripken started. He played the first 27
games (beginning on May 30, 1982) mostly at third
base, and all the rest at shortstop.

10.2 A. Tommy John John pitched 26 seasons (1963-74,
1976-87) for the Indians, White Sox, Dodgers,
Yankees, Angels, and A's. He compiled a career
record of 288-231.

10.3 A. Bobby Bonds Bonds did it five times: 1969 (32
home runs, 45 stolen bases), 1973 (39, 43), 1975 (32,
30), 1977 (37, 41), and 1978 (31, 43). Canseco
became the first-ever member of the "40-40" club in
1988, but so far has had no other "30-30" season.
Johnson and Mays each were members of the club
twice (and Johnson is still active).

10.4 B. Yogi Berra Berra won pennants managing the
Yankees in 1964 and the Mets in 1973. Anderson did
it too, but later. He won pennants for Cincinnati in
1970, 1972, 1973, 1975, and 1976, and for Detroit in
1984 and 1987, and even won the World Series in
both leagues (1975, 1976, 1984). Huggins and
Stengel both managed in the National League prior to
managing the Yankees to pennants; but in five
seasons with St. Louis (1913-17), Huggins's team
never finished better than third place, and Stengel's
Dodgers, Braves, and Mets (1934-43, 1962-65) never
finished higher than fifth. McCarthy, by the way, did
it in the National League with Chicago in 1929, and
in the American League with New York in 1932 (and
seven more times, through 1943).

10.5 **D. Texas**   Staub did play for Texas, but had just 102
hits for them (in 109 games). The fourth team for
which he had more than 500 hits was the New York
Mets. Staub is also the only player to play in at least
500 games for each of four different teams. He
played the most for the Mets (942 games, in 1972-75
and 1981-85).

10.6 **B. second base**   Although he came up as a second
baseman for Cincinnati in 1963, he played only 628
games there. He played 634 games at third, 948 at
first, and 1,327 in the outfield. And if left and right
field are counted as distinct positions, Rose is the
only player ever to play 500 or more at each of *five*
different positions—and also the only player to start
at five different positions in All-Star Games.

10.7 **C. 50**   After 50 straight successful attempts, he was
finally thrown out by Nelson Santovenia of the
Montreal Expos. The American League record is 32,
held by both Willie Wilson of the Royals (1980) and
Julio Cruz of Seattle (1980-81).

10.8 **A. Luis Aparicio**   Aparicio led the league in stolen
bases every year from 1956-64. He set major league
records for a shortstop for games (2,581), assists
(8,016), and double plays (1,553). He also set
American League shortstop records for chances
(12,564) and putouts (4,548).

10.9 **A. Walt Alston**   While managing the Dodgers to seven
World Series, he also managed eight All-Star Games
and won all but one. He was the first manager of the
1970s to be inducted into the Hall of Fame.

10.10 **D. Brooks Robinson**   Robinson played 23 years for
Baltimore from 1955-77. Kaline (Detroit), Ott (New
York Giants), and Musial (St. Louis) each had 22
years of service with a single club.

10.11 **C. 3**   Williams won pennants with the Boston Red Sox
(in 1967, in his first year as a manager), the Oakland

A's (1972, 1973), and the San Diego Padres (1984).
He also managed for California, Montreal, and
Seattle, and he retired in 1988.

10.12 **C. Gary Carter**   On June 19, 1990, playing for San
Francisco, Carter caught his 1,862nd game, passing
Al Lopez. Carter now stands fifth on the all-time list
of major league games caught behind Bob Boone,
Carlton Fisk, Lopez (who caught some games on the
American League to go with his former record
National League total), and Jim Sundberg.

10.13 **C. Ty Cobb**   Of his 892 stolen bases, Cobb stole home
50 times.

10.14 **B. Curt Flood**   From September 3, 1965 through June
4, 1967, Flood handled 568 chances in 227 games
without making an error. But Puhl (Houston, 1977-)
owns the highest lifetime fielding percentage for an
outfielder, a .993 mark, a sizable .002 higher than
that of the next best outfielders.

10.15 **C. Cal Ripken Jr.**   After making an error on April 14,
1990, the Baltimore shortstop handled 431
consecutive chances—also a record for the
position—without making another one. His streak
finally ended on July 28, in the fifth inning of a game
against Kansas City. The previous record of 88
consecutive games without an error had been set by
Kevin Elster of the Mets during the 1988-89 seasons.

10.16 **C. 18**   Billy Martin alone accounted for five of these
hirings (in 1975, 1979, 1983, 1985, and 1987). Bob
Lemon was hired twice (1978 and 1981), as were
Gene Michael (1980 and 1982) and Lou Piniella
(1985 and 1988). Dick Howser (1979), Clyde King
(1982), Yogi Berra (1983), Dallas Green (1988), and
Bucky Dent (1989) were the others given the job
(besides Virdon and Merrill).
       But in 1990, George Steinbrenner, the Yankee
owner responsible for all the managerial changes,
extended Merrill's contract through 1992, as one of his

final acts before being forced by Commissioner Fay Vincent to step down as Yankee owner (for "conduct not in the best interests of baseball," relating to Steinbrenner's dealings with a "known gambler").

10.17 **C. Phil Niekro**   Niekro is credited with 83 double plays. Spahn has the National League record of 82, and Lemon the American League record of 78. Fitzsimmons had a total of 79 for the Dodgers and Giants from 1925-43.

10.18 **A. 2**   Only Tris Speaker, with 139, and Ty Cobb, with 107, reached that level.

10.19 **D. Leo Durocher**   Durocher managed 24 years (1939-55, 1966-73) for Brooklyn, the New York Giants, the Chicago Cubs, and Houston. Anson managed in the National League for 20 years (1879-98, for Chicago and New York), Boudreau for 16 years in the American League (1942-50, 1952-57, 1960, for Cleveland, Boston, Kansas City, and Chicago), and Cronin in the American League for 15 (1933-47, for Washington and Boston).

10.20 **B. Stan Musial**   Cobb managed Detroit from 1921-26; Ott managed the New York Giants from 1942-48; and Young very briefly managed Boston in the American League (seven games in 1907).

10.21 **B. Gil Hodges**   Hodges made 326 putouts, and also holds the record for most games played at first (38). He played in the Series for Brooklyn in 1949, 1952-53, 1955-56, and 1959.

10.22 **A. Yogi Berra**   From 1949-61, Berra had 61 putouts. Mays had 55 (1954-68, 1970-72), the outfield record, Gehrig had 53 (1933-38), the most by a first baseman, and Robinson had 11, the most by a third baseman.

10.23 **D. pitcher**   The record is 385, by Paul Lindblad (playing for the A's and Texas, from the first game of a doubleheader on August 27, 1966 to April 30, 1974). During the streak, he handled 126 chances in all. Pitchers, of course, handle fewer chances than players at other positions. The record for catchers is 159 games, by Rick Cerone (Yankees and Boston, July 5, 1987 to May 8, 1989), with 896 chances in all. For first base, it's 193 games, by Steve Garvey (San Diego, June 26, 1983, second game, to April 14, 1985), 1,623 chances. The record for outfielders is 266 games, by Don Demeter (Philadelphia and Detroit, September 3, 1962, first game, to July 6, 1965), with 449 chances in all.

10.24 **C. shortstop**   The record for shortstops is 95 games and, until 1990, was 88 (see question 10.15). For catchers, the record is 159 games (see previous question). The record for second basemen is 123 consecutive errorless games, accomplished by Ryne Sandberg of the Cubs in his last 90 games in 1989 and his first 33 games in 1990. (Until Sandberg's streak, the record for a second baseman was just 91 consecutive errorless games, set by Joe Morgan, while playing for Cincinnati, 1977-78.) And for third basemen, it's 97 games, a record set by Jim Davenport (San Francisco, July 29, 1966 to April 28, 1968).

10.25 **C. third base**   The best season fielding average for a third baseman is .989 (Don Money, Milwaukee Brewers, 1974). For a second baseman, the record is .997, by Bobby Grich, California, in 1985 and for a shortstop, it's .992 by Tony Fernandez, Toronto, 1989. Though rare, perfect 1.000 fielding percentages have been recorded for a season of 100 games or more at first base (Steve Garvey for San Diego, 1984), catcher (Buddy Rosar for the Philadelphia Athletics, 1946), pitcher (Walter Johnson for Washington, 1913, and Randy Jones for San Diego, 1976), and outfield (many; those doing it in 150 or more games are Danny Litwhiler for the Philadelphia Phillies, 1942; Rocky Colavito for Cleveland, 1965; Curt Flood for St. Louis, 1966; Terry Puhl for Houston, 1979; and Brian Downing for California, 1982).

Chapter 11

Odds and Ends

This chapter contains all the questions that didn't fit anywhere else. Instead of statistics, this quiz is devoted to all sorts of baseball miscellany, from baseball brothers to early retirees to rules that the official scorer follows. (Answers and explanations begin on page 117.)

11.1 About how much water (or equivalent liquids) do trainers advise players to drink during a game?
   A. not more than half a quart per nine innings
   B. 5 ounces before a game and every hour thereafter
   C. 10 ounces before a game and every 20 minutes thereafter
   D. 20 ounces before a game and every half inning thereafter

11.2 Who is, or was, Katie Casey?
   A. Casey's wife in the poem "Casey at the Bat"
   B. the main character in the song "Take Me Out to the Ball Game"
   C. the first female owner of a major league team
   D. the mascot of the old Kansas City Athletics

11.3 What happened on 8/8/88 at Chicago's Wrigley Field?
A. Exactly 8,888 fans showed up at the park.
B. A helicopter made an emergency landing in the infield.
C. Nolan Ryan struck out his 5,000th batter.
D. The stadium's first-ever scheduled night game was washed out by thunderstorms.

11.4 Before becoming a well-known actor, who was the public address announcer for the Brooklyn Dodgers at Ebbets Field during the 1938 and 1939 seasons?
A. Gene Barry
B. Buddy Ebsen
C. John Forsythe
D. Ronald Reagan

11.5 If a player comes to the plate just once during a game, which of the following results will bring to an end any consecutive-game hitting streak he had entering the game?
A. He is hit by a pitch.
B. He makes a sacrifice bunt.
C. He makes a sacrifice fly.
D. He walks.

11.6 In what stadium was the American League one-game attendance record set?
A. Anaheim Stadium
B. Cleveland Stadium
C. Seattle Kingdome
D. Yankee Stadium

11.7 Which of the following never happened?
A. Phil and Joe Niekro opposed each other as starting pitchers.
B. Tony and Billy Conigliaro each played in more than 100 games in the same year for the Boston Red Sox.
C. All three Alou brothers—Felipe, Matty and Jesus—played in the outfield for the same team in the same game.
D. All three DiMaggio brothers—Joe, Dom, and Vince—played in the same All-Star Game.

11.8 Which statement is false?
A. Ernie Banks was the first black player on the Cubs.
B. Elston Howard was the first black player on the Yankees.
C. Willie Mays was the first black player on the Giants.
D. Ozzie Virgil was the first black player on the Tigers.

11.9 Quite a few major league hitters have been lefthanded batters but righthanded throwers. Which of these lefthanded hitters threw lefthanded?
A. Ty Cobb
B. Roger Maris
C. Stan Musial
D. Ted Williams

11.10 The monuments in Yankee Stadium, once in play in left centerfield but now out of play in Monument Park in left, memorialize all but which of the following persons?
A. Lou Gehrig
B. Miller Huggins
C. Joe McCarthy
D. Babe Ruth

11.11 Which pair of major league players were father and son?
A. Bobby Bonds and Barry Bonds
B. George Burns and George Burns
C. Bob Meusel and Irish Meusel
D. Frank Snyder and Duke Snider

11.12 What Hall of Famer tragically choked to death on a piece of meat at age 59?
A. Jimmy Foxx
B. Hank Greenberg
C. Christy Mathewson
D. Joe Medwick

11.13 What two players, along with a minor leaguer, were traded by the A's to the Orioles in 1976 in exchange for Don Baylor, Mike Torrez, and Paul Mitchell?
A. Paul Blair and Tippy Martinez
B. Bobby Bonds and Doug DeCinces
C. Ken Holtzman and Reggie Jackson
D. Hal McRae and Ken Singleton

11.14 Which of these players was the youngest when he played his final major league game?
    A. Ralph Kiner
    B. Sandy Koufax
    C. Tony Kubek
    D. Denny McLain

11.15 What do Andy Messersmith and Dave McNally have in common?
    A. Each lost two games in the 1974 World Series.
    B. They played on the same teams in Little League, high school, and college.
    C. They share the record for most errors in an inning by a pitcher.
    D. They tested the reserve clause by playing 1975 without contracts, and were the first players to become free agents that way.

11.16 In baseball slang, what does the term "nickel curve" refer to?
    A. a curve that breaks sharply just as it reaches the plate
    B. a curve that is ineffective
    C. a curve thrown with all five fingers gripping the ball
    D. a slider

11.17 Which team plays its home games in the SkyDome?
    A. Milwaukee
    B. Minnesota
    C. Seattle
    D. Toronto

11.18 What hitter, like Babe Ruth, began his major league career as a lefthanded pitcher, and posted a 4-4 record his first year?
    A. Lou Gehrig
    B. Reggie Jackson
    C. Lefty O'Doul
    D. George Sisler

11.19 Why are some 1909 Honus Wagner baseball cards now worth over $100,000 each?

   A. Most of them were accidentally destroyed in a fire before being shipped from the warehouse.

   B. The printer changed the plate midway through the year and used a picture of Wagner with a young Babe Ruth on a few of the cards.

   C. They contain an error in which Wagner's picture is printed upside down.

   D. Wagner objected to having his picture on the card and got the company to withdraw it.

11.20 A pitcher who finishes up a game for the winning team, but who himself is not the winning pitcher, would earn a save in all but which of the following situations?

   A. He enters the game leading 3-0 and pitches the entire ninth inning.

   B. He enters the game leading 4-0 and pitches the entire eighth and ninth innings.

   C. He enters the game leading 5-0 and pitches the entire seventh, eighth and ninth innings.

   D. He enters the game with two outs in the ninth, the bases loaded, an 0-2 count on the batter, and a lead of 5-0.

11.21 Cecil Fielder had an outstanding year for Detroit in 1990, but he played for a different team the year before. Which one?

   A. Hanshin Tigers

   B. Lakeland Tigers

   C. Toronto Blue Jays

   D. Yakult Swallows

11.22 How tall was the tallest player in major league history?

   A. 6' 6"

   B. 6' 8"

   C. 6' 10"

   D. 7'

11.23 Which of the following requirements for qualifying for a season fielding championship is incorrect?
  A. A catcher must catch in half his team's games.
  B. An infielder must play in at least two-thirds of his team's games.
  C. An outfielder must play in at least two-thirds of his team's games.
  D. A starting pitcher must pitch in at least one-ninth of his team's games.

11.24 What player, who was the first to appear in both a Rose Bowl and World Series, had his career shortened because of his fear of flying?
  A. Hank Greenberg
  B. Jackie Jensen
  C. Don Larsen
  D. Bobby Shantz

11.25 From what word or name does the term "sabermetrics" derive?
  A. an acronym for the Society for American Baseball Research (SABR)
  B. pitcher Bret Saberhagen
  C. the Spanish word *saber*, meaning "knowledge" or "to know"
  D. the word "saber," a weapon that can be swung like a bat

Answers and Explanations

11.1 **C. 10 ounces before a game and every 20 minutes thereafter** Dehydration can take a serious toll on athletic performance. Most players drink water during games, but some prefer such liquids as Gatorade Thirst Quencher (a Quaker Oats product) or Exceed (distributed by Ross Labs).

11.2 **B. the main character in the song "Take me Out to the Ball Game"** Her name appears in the full verse, but not in the well-known chorus that begins "Take me out to the ball game." The chorus explains where "baseball mad" Katie tells her young beau she wants to go on a date, rather than to a show. The song was written in 1908 by Jack Norworth and Albert von Tilzer, neither of whom had ever even seen a major league baseball game.

11.3 **D. The stadium's first-ever scheduled night game was washed out by thunderstorms.** As a result of the storm, Wrigley's first official night game was played on August 9, when the Cubs defeated the Mets 6-4. Lights were almost installed at Wrigley in 1941, but wound up being given to the war effort.

11.4 **C. John Forsythe** Forsythe, of course, went on to star in TV's *Bachelor Father* and *Dynasty*, and was the voice of Charlie in *Charlie's Angels*. As part of a June 1, 1990 celebration of the 100th anniversary of the Dodgers' franchise, Forsythe introduced the players at Dodger Stadium and announced from the public address box during the first inning.

11.5 **C. He makes a sacrifice fly.** Under current scoring rules, a sacrifice fly will end the streak. One other way a player can fail to hit but keep his streak alive is to be awarded first base on defensive interference.

11.6 **B. Cleveland Stadium** Cleveland had record

attendance of 86,288 for an October 10, 1948 World Series game against Boston. Currently, Cleveland has the largest capacity of any major league stadium (77,797).

11.7 **D. All three DiMaggio brothers—Joe, Dom, and Vince—played in the same All-Star Game.** Vince's two All-Star Games came in 1943 and 1944, years in which his brothers were out of baseball because of military service. Dom and Joe were both chosen as All-Stars several times, and played together in the outfield on three of those occasions. Overall, Joe was chosen 13 times (1936-42, 1946-51), and Dom 7 times (1941-42, 1946, 1949-52).

The Niekros opposed each other as starting pitchers nine times, the first being July 5, 1967, when Joe was with the Cubs and Phil with the Braves. In 1970, Tony Conigliaro played in 146 games, and his brother Billy in 114, for the Red Sox. (That year, their combined home run total of 54—36 for Tony, 18 for Billy—set a single-season record for two brothers on the same team.) The three Alous all played in the same outfield for the Giants on September 15, 1963, necessitating the "benching" of Willie Mays.

11.8 **C. Willie Mays was the first black player on the Giants.**   Hank Thompson had joined the Giants in 1949 after being with the St. Louis Browns in 1947; Mays was a rookie in 1951. Banks joined the Cubs in 1953, Howard joined the Yankees in 1955, and Virgil joined the Tigers in 1958.

11.9 **C. Stan Musial**   Lefthanded throwers who bat righthanded are much rarer; a notable example is Rickey Henderson.

11.10 **C. Joe McCarthy**   McCarthy managed the Yankees to seven championships in the 1930s and 1940s—a record shared with Casey Stengel—and has the highest winning percentage of any manager in baseball history (.614). But the first three monuments were built to memorialize earlier Yankees, including manager Miller Huggins, who led them into six World Series in the 1920s. Later, a plaque was added for Yankee catcher Thurman Munson, who died in a plane crash in 1979 after helping the Yankees to three straight pennants.

11.11 **A. Bobby Bonds and Barry Bonds**   And when Barry Bonds hit 30 home runs and stole 30 bases in 1990 en route to winning the National League Most Valuable Player award, he made himself and his father the only father-son combination to have both been members of the "30-30 club." The two George Burnses were contemporaries, one playing in the National League from 1911-25 (leading the league in stolen bases in 1914 and 1919), the other in the American League from 1914-29 (winning the MVP award in 1926), and they were unrelated. Bob and Irish (real name Emil) Meusel were brothers, and faced each other in the 1921-23 World Series (Bob playing for the Yankees, Irish for the Giants). Frank Snyder was about the right age to have been Duke Snider's father, and Snider *could* have changed the spelling of his name—but it isn't so. The two were unrelated.

In 1990, Ken Griffey and Ken Griffey Jr. became the first father-son combination to play on the same team, after Griffey Sr. was signed by the Mariners when the Reds placed him on waivers.

11.12 **A. Jimmy Foxx**   It happened in July, 1967, while he was dining with his brother. Mathewson died of tuberculosis in 1925, at the age of 47. Medwick (1911-75) lived to be 63, and Greenberg (1911-86) lived to be 75.

11.13 **C. Ken Holtzman and Reggie Jackson**   None of the players in the trade stayed long with their new teams. Midway through the 1976 season, Holtzman was traded to the Yankees as part of a 10-player trade. His totals for the year were fairly good (14-11, 3.65 ERA), but in the next three years he had an overall record of 9-15, mostly with the Cubs, before retiring.

Jackson batted .277 with 27 home runs for Baltimore
in 1976, but then signed with the Yankees as a free
agent. (He stayed with the Yankees from 1977-81,
during which he helped them to three pennants.)
Baylor, after a so-so year in 1976 (.247, 15 home
runs), left Oakland and signed as a free agent with
California. Torrez had a good year pitching for the
A's in 1976 (he won 16, lost 12, 2.50 ERA), but was
traded from the A's to the Yankees in early 1977, then
signed with Boston as a free agent at the end of that
season. Mitchell was 9-7 with a 4.25 ERA in 1976,
was sold to Seattle the following year, and never
again had a winning season.

11.14   **D. Denny McLain**   After two suspensions by
Commissioner Bowie Kuhn in 1970—one for
bookmaking and one for gun possession—the man
who had won 31 games in 1968 and 24 more in 1969
fell to a record of 3-5. The following year, he was
10-22, and his career ended after a 1972 record of 4-7
when he was 28 1/2. The other three players retired
early because of fairly serious physical problems:
Kiner's bad back forced him out at age 32 (after the
1955 season), an arthritic pitching elbow felled
Koufax at 30 (after 1966), and a spinal problem
sidelined Kubek at 28 (after 1965), though he was
nearly 29, and several months older than McLain was
in his last game.

11.15   **D. They tested the reserve clause by playing 1975
without contracts, and were the first players to
become free agents that way.**   After their 1975
noncontract seasons, arbitrator Peter Seitz agreed
with them that they were no longer bound to their
teams.
        Both were in postseason play in 1974, by the way.
Messersmith was 1-0 for Los Angeles in the LCS and
0-2 in the World Series; McNally was 0-1 for
Baltimore in the League Championship Series, but
never made it to the World Series because Oakland
won the LCS. And in case you were wondering, the
modern record for errors by a pitcher in one inning is

three, by Tommy John (Yankees)—all on one batted ball—on July 27, 1988, in the fourth inning. Before 1901, Cy Seymour also made three errors in an inning on May 21, 1898, in the sixth inning, pitching for the New York Giants.

11.16 **B. a curve that is ineffective** It's too slow, or just doesn't break much—that is, not worth a plugged nickel.

11.17 **D. Toronto** The stadium opened in June 1989. One of its noteworthy features is its 150' x 35' scoreboard, the largest in baseball. Milwaukee plays in County Stadium, Minnesota plays in the Hubert H. Humphrey Metrodome, and Seattle plays in the Kingdome.

11.18 **D. George Sisler** Sisler was 4-4 for the St. Louis Browns in 1915, his first year in the majors, and threw a 1–0 shutout over Walter Johnson on September 17, 1916, as part of a 1-2 record that year. By then, though, he was already playing regularly as a first baseman. Over the next few years, he made six scattered relief appearances, saving three games. O'Doul, who posted a .349 lifetime batting average while playing from 1919-23 and 1928-34 (for New York and Boston of the American League and for New York, Philadelphia, and Brooklyn of the National League), did begin his minor league career as a pitcher, but had early arm trouble and was only 1-1 lifetime in the majors. Neither Gehrig nor Jackson ever made a major league pitching appearance, although Gehrig pitched in college for Columbia and won one game for Hartford in the minors.

11.19 **D. Wagner objected to having his picture on the card and got the company to withdraw it.** Whether he threatened to sue, or simply paid the company some cash, is unclear—but it is believed that fewer than 100 of the cards exist today. According to a popular story, Wagner objected to the card because he did not want to seem to be promoting smoking. He did chew tobacco, though, and also appeared on some other tobacco cards—so another story, to the effect that he wanted the company to pay him, may be more accurate.

11.20 **B. He enters the game leading 4-0 and pitches the entire 8th and 9th innings.**   To earn a save under current rules, a pitcher must finish the game for the winning team, not himself be the winning pitcher, and do one of the following: enter the game with a lead of no more than three runs and pitch at least one inning; enter the game with the potential tying run either on base, at bat, or on deck (the count on the current batter is irrelevant); or pitch effectively for at least three innings.

11.21 **A. Hanshin Tigers**   For the Tigers of Japan's Central League, Fielder hit 38 home runs in 1989—13 fewer than he hit in 1990, when he became the first American Leaguer to hit 50 home runs since Roger Maris and Mickey Mantle did it in 1961. He had been only a part-time player for the Blue Jays from 1985-88 before being sold to the Japanese team.

11.22 **C. 6′ 10″**   Randy Johnson, who began his career in 1988 as a pitcher for Montreal and was traded to Seattle the following year, is the tallest major leaguer ever. He pitched a no-hitter on June 2, 1990.

11.23 **D. A starting pitcher must pitch in at least one-ninth of his team's games.**   A pitcher—whether a starter, reliever, or both—must have at least as many innings pitched as his team has games. Exceptions are made for pitchers who handle more chances in the field than other qualifiers.

11.24 **B. Jackie Jensen**   Jensen played from 1950-61 for the Yankees, Senators, and Red Sox, winning the Most Valuable Player award while playing for Boston in 1958. He played in the Rose Bowl in 1949 as an All-American running back at California (his team

lost 20-14 to Northwestern) and in the 1950 World
Series for the Yankees (the Yankees beat the Phillies
four games to none).

11.25   **A.   an acronym for the Society for American Baseball
       Research (SABR)**   Sabermetrics refers to a search
       for objective baseball knowledge by SABR members
       interested in statistical analysis. Readers of such
       books as *The Bill James Baseball Abstracts*, by Bill
       James, or *The Hidden Game of Baseball* and *Total
       Baseball*, both by John Thorn and Pete Palmer, will
       be very familiar with it. Not satisfied with measuring
       player performances on the basis of traditional
       statistics, sabermetricians try to find new, more
       meaningful ways to evaluate how players are doing.
       Since the rise of sabermetrics in the 1980s, attention
       has been focused on many new kinds of stats, such as
       "batting average in late-inning pressure situations,"
       "runs created," and "linear weights."

Chapter 12

Envelope, Please

Being recognized as a good player is nice, but such glory is often fleeting. An award or special honor, though—whether a home run crown, an MVP award, or a Gold Glove—stays with a player forever. And the personal goal of many a young player is to win baseball's highest honor: being elected to the Hall of Fame. (Answers and explanations begin on page 130.)

12.1 In the first balloting to select members of the Hall of Fame, what player received the most votes?
A. Ty Cobb
B. Walter Johnson
C. Babe Ruth
D. Honus Wagner

12.2 Although rules are sometimes waived, which of the following is *not* ordinarily required for a player to be elected to the Hall of Fame?
A. He must have played at least 10 seasons.
B. He must have been retired for 5 years.
C. He must not have received a lifetime suspension from baseball.
D. He must receive votes on at least 75 percent of the ballots.

12.3 Who was the youngest player ever to be inducted into the Hall of Fame?
- **A.** Roy Campanella
- **B.** Sandy Koufax
- **C.** Mickey Mantle
- **D.** Babe Ruth

12.4 Which award has been in existence the fewest years?
- **A.** Cy Young
- **B.** Gold Glove
- **C.** Most Valuable Player
- **D.** Rookie of the Year

12.5 Which of these pitchers won the most Cy Young awards?
- **A.** Steve Carlton
- **B.** Sandy Koufax
- **C.** Jim Palmer
- **D.** Tom Seaver

12.6 Who was the first pitcher to win Cy Young awards in both leagues?
- **A.** Jim Bunning
- **B.** Jim Kaat
- **C.** Gaylord Perry
- **D.** Don Sutton

12.7 What catcher won a record 10 Gold Glove awards?
- **A.** Johnny Bench
- **B.** Bob Boone
- **C.** Gary Carter
- **D.** Carlton Fisk

12.8 Who, along with Brooks Robinson, shares the record for winning the most Gold Glove awards at any position?
- **A.** Luis Aparicio
- **B.** Keith Hernandez
- **C.** Jim Kaat
- **D.** Mike Schmidt

12.9 Who, along with Roberto Clemente, shares the record of winning the most Gold Glove awards as an outfielder?
  A. Curt Flood
  B. Al Kaline
  C. Willie Mays
  D. Amos Otis

12.10 The annual Roberto Clemente award is given in recognition of what?
  A. achievements on and off the field
  B. most assists by an outfielder
  C. most hits in a season
  D. on-field leadership

12.11 Who was the first American Leaguer to win the annual Outstanding Designated Hitter award three times?
  A. Don Baylor
  B. Willie Horton
  C. Greg Luzinski
  D. Hal McRae

12.12 What team's players have won the Most Valuable Player award the most times?
  A. Dodgers
  B. Giants
  C. Reds
  D. Yankees

12.13 Since 1989, a rookie must meet *all but which* of these qualifications in order to be eligible to win the Rookie of the Year award?
  A. He must not have been on a major league roster for 45 or more days in a previous season.
  B. He must not have played more than 100 games as a professional player in Japan.
  C. If a nonpitcher, he must not have had as many as 130 at-bats in a previous season.
  D. If a pitcher, he must not have pitched as many as 50 innings in a previous season.

12.14 In which of these years did Ted Williams win the Most
Valuable Player award?
- **A.** 1941, when he batted .406 and led the league in home
  runs with 37
- **B.** 1942, when he won the Triple Crown with a .356
  average, 36 home runs, and 137 RBIs
- **C.** 1946, when he batted .342 with 38 home runs and
  123 RBIs, none of which were league-leading totals
- **D.** 1947, when he won the Triple Crown with a .343
  average, 32 home runs, and 114 RBIs

12.15 Who won a Rookie of the Year award despite making 41
errors?
- **A.** Dick Allen
- **B.** John Castino
- **C.** Jackie Robinson
- **D.** Steve Sax

12.16 Which of the following players won a Rookie of the Year
award?
- **A.** Hank Aaron
- **B.** Jose Canseco
- **C.** Mickey Mantle
- **D.** Jim Rice

12.17 Who was the first player to win the Rookie of the Year
award as a designated hitter?
- **A.** Harold Baines
- **B.** Alvin Davis
- **C.** Hal McRae
- **D.** Eddie Murray

12.18 In 1987, the Rookie of the Year award was renamed for
what player ?
- **A.** Ty Cobb
- **B.** Ken Hubbs
- **C.** Jackie Robinson
- **D.** Roy Sievers

12.19 Who was the first relief pitcher to win the Most Valuable
Player award?
  A. Roy Face
  B. Rollie Fingers
  C. Willie Hernandez
  D. Jim Konstanty

12.20 Who was the first relief pitcher to win the American
League Cy Young award?
  A. Rollie Fingers
  B. Willie Hernandez
  C. Sparky Lyle
  D. Hoyt Wilhelm

12.21 Among players elected to the Hall of Fame, what last
name is the most common?
  A. Gibson
  B. Johnson
  C. Robinson
  D. Williams

12.22 In 1950, both leagues' Rookie of the Year awards went to
players from the same city. What was the city?
  A. Boston
  B. Chicago
  C. New York
  D. St. Louis

12.23 Who is the only non-New York Yankee to win three
American League Most Valuable Player awards?
  A. Rod Carew
  B. Jimmy Foxx
  C. Hank Greenberg
  D. Carl Yastrzemski

12.24 Who was the first National League player ever to win
three Most Valuable Player awards?
  A. Johnny Bench
  B. Roy Campanella
  C. Stan Musial
  D. Mike Schmidt

12.25 Who was the first foreign athlete to receive the Polish
government's highest sports award, the Merited
Champions Medal?
   A. Ted Kluszewski
   B. Stan Musial
   C. Tom Paciorek
   D. Al Simmons

Answers and Explanations

12.1 **A. Ty Cobb**   Cobb received votes from 222 of the 226 members of the Baseball Writers Association of America polled. (The BBWAA still elects Hall of Fame members.) Ruth and Wagner were tied for second, with 215 votes each.

12.2 **C. He must not have received a lifetime suspension from baseball.**   There is no rule that states that a lifetime suspension will keep a player out of the Hall of Fame—though as a practical matter, it could—and so far has, for Joe Jackson, because of his lifetime ban that resulted from the Chicago "Black Sox" scandal. Many sportswriters have said they are having trouble deciding whether Commissioner Bart Giamatti's suspension of Pete Rose for gambling will prevent them from voting him into the Hall when he becomes eligible.

An example of the suspension of the usual waiting period occurred when Roberto Clemente was elected to the Hall of Fame in 1973, the year after his untimely death in an airplane crash.

12.3 **B. Sandy Koufax**   After retiring at age 31 because of arm trouble (he pitched his last game at age 30), he was elected to the Hall of Fame at age 36, in his first year of eligibility after the usual five-year waiting period. Lou Gehrig also was 36 when he was selected in December 1939, but he was several months older than Koufax.

12.4 **B. Gold Glove**   Gold Glove awards have been given by *The Sporting News* since 1957. The other three awards are determined by votes of the Baseball Writers Association of America. The Cy Young award has been given since 1956, Rookie of the Year awards since 1947, and Most Valuable Player awards since 1931. Prior to the BBWAA's involvement, there were two earlier versions of the MVP award: the Chalmers awards (1911-14), in which winners won a new car, and League MVP awards (1922-29).

12.5 **A.** **Steve Carlton** Carlton won a record four (1972, 1977, 1980, 1982), and was the first ever to win on a last-place team (the Phillies, in 1972). Koufax won in 1963, 1965, and 1966—a more remarkable feat than Carlton's, really, because only one award was given in each of those years (beginning in 1967, one award was given in each league). Palmer and Seaver each won three as well: Palmer in 1973, 1975, and 1976, and Seaver in 1969, 1973, and 1975.

12.6 **C.** **Gaylord Perry** Perry won for both Cleveland in 1972 and San Diego in 1978.

12.7 **A.** **Johnny Bench** Bench's lifetime fielding average was .990, which is not quite good enough to be among the top 10 of all time—a group that is led by Bill Freehan, Elston Howard, and Jim Sundberg, each at .993.

12.8 **C.** **Jim Kaat** Kaat won 16 straight Gold Gloves as a pitcher from 1962-77. (The next best total by any pitcher is Bob Gibson's 9.) Robinson, as a third baseman, also won his 16 consecutively, from 1960-75. For the record, Aparicio won 9 Gold Glove awards, Hernandez 11, and Schmidt 10.

12.9 **C.** **Willie Mays** Clemente and Mays each won 12. Kaline had the next best total of 10.

12.10 **A.** **achievements on and off the field** It is given to "the player who best exemplifies the game of baseball on and off the field"; and since most major leaguers are pretty good on the field, the emphasis is really on off-the-field achievements. In 1990, Dave Stewart of the A's won, the twentieth time the award was given. He got it for helping various charitable organizations, such as the Cystic Fibrosis Foundation and MS Society, and for helping rescue workers and people left homeless after the Bay Area earthquake

during the 1989 World Series. The award is aptly
named, since Clemente died in a plane crash on
December 31, 1972, while trying to bring supplies to
earthquake victims in Managua, Nicaragua.

12.11   **D.   Hal McRae**   Hal McRae won it in 1976, 1980, and
1982, playing for the Kansas City Royals. Baylor
(while playing for for New York and Boston), Horton
(Detroit and Seattle), and Luzinski (Chicago) won the
award twice each, as has Harold Baines (Chicago).

12.12   **D.   Yankees**   Yankee players have won a total of 20.
The winners (and their number of awards) are: Babe
Ruth (1), Lou Gehrig (2), Joe DiMaggio (3), Joe
Gordon (1), Spud Chandler (1), Phil Rizzuto (1),
Yogi Berra (3), Mickey Mantle (3), Roger Maris (2),
Elston Howard (1), Thurman Munson (1), Don
Mattingly (1). Ruth's award and one of Gehrig's were
League awards, awarded before the BBWAA made
the MVP awards their responsibility. Gehrig also
won *The Sporting News* MVP award in 1931 and
1934, when he was passed over by the BBWAA.

12.13   **B.   He must not have played more than 100 games as
a professional player in Japan.**   There is no
requirement regarding service in Japan or any other
foreign country. Only prior major league experience
is considered.

12.14   **C.   1946, when he batted .342 with 38 home runs and
123 RBIs, none of which were league-leading
totals**   He also led the league in runs and walks that
year—but then, he also did so in 1941, 1942, and
1947. In 1941 and 1946, the award went to New York
outfielder Joe DiMaggio, and in 1942, it went to New
York second baseman Joe Gordon. Williams did win
a second MVP in 1949, when he missed a third Triple
Crown by a fraction of a batting average point; his
numbers that year were .343 (a slightly "worse" .343
than Detroit's George Kell's), 43 home runs, and 159
RBIs.

12.15 **A. Dick Allen** Known then as Richie Allen, he committed 41 errors at third base for the Phillies in 1964. His abysmal .908 fielding average was the worst for a third baseman since 1914—but he more than made up for it with a .318 batting average, 29 home runs, and 91 RBIs.

12.16 **B. Jose Canseco** Canseco did in 1986, despite striking out 175 times. He batted only .240, but had 33 home runs and 117 RBIs. Aaron's rookie year, 1954, was not one of his best: In 122 games, he hit .280 with 13 home runs, and Wally Moon (.304, 12 home runs) of St. Louis won the award instead. When Mantle was a rookie (1951), he hit .267 and 13 home runs (in just 341 at-bats), and his teammate Gil McDougald (.306, 14 home runs) won—though Minnie Minoso, who hit .326 with 10 home runs and a league-leading 31 stolen bases, got the one awarded by *The Sporting News*. In 1975, Rice hit .309 with 22 home runs and 102 RBIs, but also lost out to a teammate, Fred Lynn, who hit .331 with 21 home runs and 105 RBIs.

12.17 **D. Eddie Murray** Murray did it playing for Baltimore in 1977. Neither Baines nor McRae was a regular DH during his rookie season, and Davis won the Rookie of the Year award in 1984 as Seattle's first baseman.

12.18 **C. Jackie Robinson** Robinson was the first winner of the Rookie of the Year award when it was instituted in 1947. (Sievers became the first American League winner two years later, when awards were given in both leagues for the first time.) The renaming took place on the 40th anniversary of the award.

12.19 **D. Jim Konstanty** Konstanty did it in 1950 for the Phillies. He appeared in a 74 games that year and had a record of 16 wins, 7 losses, and 22 saves—all league-leading totals for a reliever. He also posted an ERA of 2.66. Two of the other three choices also won MVP awards as relief pitchers: Fingers in 1981, playing for Milwaukee, and Hernandez in 1984, for Detroit. Face's 1959 performance might well have won an MVP award in some years—he was 18-1 (an all-time percentage mark of .947), with 10 saves and an ERA of 2.70—but the MVP award that year went to shortstop Ernie Banks, who hit .304 with 45 home runs and a league-leading 143 RBIs.

12.20   **C. Sparky Lyle**   Lyle won it in 1977. In the National League, fireman Mike Marshall had won the Cy Young award in 1974.

12.21   **C. Robinson**   Jackie, Brooks, and Frank Robinson are all members of the Hall of Fame. The other surnames have two representatives each: Bob and Josh Gibson, Judy and Walter Johnson, and Billy and Ted Williams.

12.22   **A. Boston**   The honored players were Walt Dropo (Red Sox), who hit .322 with 34 home runs and a league-leading 144 RBIs, and Sam Jethroe (Braves), who hit .273 with 18 home runs and a major-league-leading total of 35 stolen bases. Neither player again had as good a season. (Jethroe, who was 28 years old his rookie year, had spent his best years in the Negro Leagues.) The following year, as it happens, the award again went to crosstown rivals, but in a different city: Willie Mays of the New York Giants and Gil McDougald of the New York Yankees.

12.23   **B. Jimmy Foxx**   Foxx won it for Philadelphia in 1932-33 and for Boston in 1938. Three Yankees were three-time winners: Yogi Berra (1951, 1954-55), Joe DiMaggio (1939, 1941, 1947), and Mickey Mantle (1956-57, 1962). Carew and Yastrzemski won once each (1977 and 1967, respectively).

12.24   **C. Stan Musial**   Musial did it in 1943, 1946, and 1948. Campanella (1951, 1953, 1955) and Schmidt (1980-81, 1986) were later three-time winners, and Bench won only twice (1970, 1972).

12.25   **B. Stan Musial**   Musial received the award in 1972. If you're wondering why Hall of Famer Al Simmons is a choice, it's because his real name was Aloys Szymanski, and like Musial, he was very proud of his Polish ancestry.

Chapter 13

Records No One Wanted

"To err is human," the saying goes. Some good players have off-years, and even the best players have bad days. For one reason or another, many players end up having records they would rather forget. Here's a sampling. (Answers and explanations begin on page 140.)

13.1 A major league record for losing the most consecutive games at the start of a season was set in 1988 by the Baltimore Orioles. How many did they lose before getting their first win?
A. 9
B. 13
C. 17
D. 21

13.2 The current American and National League modern records for most consecutive games lost were set or tied by teams from the same city. What is the city?
A. Boston
B. Chicago
C. New York
D. Philadelphia

13.3 Who grounded into the most double plays in history?
A. Hank Aaron
B. Stan Musial
C. Pete Rose
D. Carl Yastrzemski

13.4 Who grounded into a record 36 double plays in a single season?
A. Hank Aaron
B. Smoky Burgess
C. Jim Rice
D. Carl Yastrzemski

13.5 What is the most at-bats a player has ever had in a season in which he batted .000?
A. 20
B. 45
C. 70
D. 95

13.6 What is the modern record for most losses in a single season by a pitcher?
A. 19
B. 24
C. 29
D. 34

13.7 What is the modern record for lowest batting average by a team?
A. .172
B. .192
C. .212
D. .232

13.8 Connie Mack was the losing manager in more games than anyone else in major league history. How many games did he lose?
A. 1,025
B. 2,025
C. 3,025
D. 4,025

13.9 What is the most consecutive innings a team has ever
gone without scoring a run?
A. 24
B. 36
C. 48
D. 64

13.10 What pitcher gave up a record 50 home runs in 1986?
A. Bert Blyleven
B. Mike Krukow
C. Jack Morris
D. Phil Niekro

13.11 What major league teams are tied for the record for the
most last-place finishes?
A. Athletics and Cubs
B. Athletics and Phillies
C. White Sox and Cubs
D. White Sox and Phillies

13.12 What franchise was in existence the longest before
winning its first World Series?
A. Brooklyn Dodgers
B. Chicago Cubs
C. Chicago White Sox
D. Philadelphia Phillies

13.13 Who holds the National League record for striking out
100 or more times the most consecutive seasons?
A. Dick Allen
B. Dave Kingman
C. Mike Schmidt
D. Willie Stargell

13.14 Who holds the record for leading a league in striking out
the most times?
A. Vince DiMaggio
B. Jimmy Foxx
C. Reggie Jackson
D. Willie Stargell

13.15 Who has been caught stealing the most times of anyone?
A. Lou Brock
B. Bert Campaneris
C. Rickey Henderson
D. Willie Wilson

13.16 What is the most players left on base by one team in a nine-inning game?
A. 17
B. 20
C. 24
D. 27

13.17 Who set a modern record by walking 208 batters in a season?
A. Bob Feller
B. Bob Gibson
C. Sandy Koufax
D. Walter Johnson

13.18 What pitcher, as a batter, struck out the most times in his career?
A. Lefty Grove
B. Christy Mathewson
C. Warren Spahn
D. Cy Young

13.19 Who managed the longest without ever winning a pennant?
A. Bucky Harris
B. Connie Mack
C. Gene Mauch
D. John McGraw

13.20 Who was the losing pitcher in both the 1986 and 1988 All-Star Games?
A. Dwight Gooden
B. Nolan Ryan
C. Mike Scott
D. Fernando Valenzuela

13.21 Who was the losing pitcher in the most shutouts?
  A. Steve Carlton
  B. Walter Johnson
  C. Nolan Ryan
  D. Don Sutton

13.22 Who played on the most All-Star Game losing teams?
  A. Al Kaline
  B. Stan Musial
  C. Brooks Robinson
  D. Pete Rose

13.23 From the league's founding in 1901 through the decade of the 1980s, what American League club lost the most games?
  A. Boston
  B. Chicago
  C. Detroit
  D. Philadelphia-Kansas City-Oakland (the A's)

13.24 From the league's founding in 1876 through the decade of the 1980s, what National League club lost the most games?
  A. Boston-Milwaukee-Atlanta (the Braves)
  B. Chicago
  C. Cincinnati
  D. Philadelphia

13.25 What pitcher set a record for committing the most balks in a season in 1988?
  A. Orel Hershiser
  B. Mark Langston
  C. Dave Stewart
  D. Rick Sutcliffe

Answers and Explanations

13.1 **D. 21**   They ended up the season 54-107. And even if
their first 21 games had not counted, they would still
have lost more games than any other team in their
division (Cleveland lost 84).

13.2 **D. Philadelphia**   The Philadelphia Phillies lost a
modern major league record 23 games in a row in
1961. The American League record is 20, shared by
Boston (1906) and the Philadelphia Athletics
(accomplished twice, in 1916 and 1943).

13.3 **A. Hank Aaron**   Aaron grounded into a record 328
(305 in the National League, 23 in the American
League). The one-league record is 323, held by
Yastrzemski.

13.4 **C. Jim Rice**   Rice, with the disadvantageous
combination of being a slow runner and a
righthanded hitter, set the record in 1984, and fell one
double play short of tying his own record the
following year. Yastrzemski holds the record for a
lefthanded hitter (30, in 1964).

13.5 **C. 70**   Pitcher Bob Buhl set the record while playing for
the Braves and the Cubs in 1962. Buhl was always a
weak hitter. His lifetime average, over a period of 15
years (1953-67), was .089 (76 for 857). The American
League season record for hitless at-bats is 61,
"achieved" by Bill Wight of Chicago in 1950.

13.6 **C. 29**   Vic Willis, who had lost 25 games the year
before, went 11-29 for the 51-103 Boston Braves in
1905, though his ERA was a respectable 3.21.
Usually, pitchers who lose a lot of games are
suffering from poor batting and fielding support, as
was the case with Willis, but aren't pitching all that
badly—if they were, they wouldn't keep getting more
chances on the mound. Indeed, Willis's lifetime

record (set from 1898-1910, for the Braves, Pirates, and Cardinals) was an impressive 246-206, with an even more impressive lifetime ERA of 2.63.

13.7 **C. .212**   The Chicago White Sox hit just .212 in 1910. The National League record is .213 by Brooklyn in 1908.

13.8 **D. 4,025**   But Mack, who managed for 53 years, also has the record for being on the winning side more than any other manager—3,776 times.

13.9 **C. 48**   The Philadelphia A's were shut out for the last seven innings of a game on September 22, 1906, and did not score again until the sixth inning of a game on September 26. The record was equaled by the Chicago Cubs in 1968, when they went for the last eight innings on June 15 without scoring, and did not score again until the third inning of a game on June 21.

13.10 **A. Bert Blyleven**   Pitching for Minnesota, Blyleven also led the league in innings pitched that year, with 272. His season won-lost record was 17-14, with 215 strikeouts and a 4.01 ERA.

13.11 **B. Athletics and Phillies**   The Athletics (Philadelphia, Kansas City, and Oakland) and the Philadelphia Phillies have each finished in last place 24 times.

13.12 **D. Philadelphia Phillies**   Since the modern World Series began in 1903, the Phillies waited 77 years for their first world championship, when they defeated Kansas City, four games to two, in the 1980 World Series. They had reached the Series in 1915 and 1950, but lost both times.

13.13 **D. Willie Stargell**   Stargell did it 12 times in a row, from 1965-76, for Pittsburgh. He also did it in 1979, for a National League record total of 13 (though he only led the league in strikeouts once, when he had 154 in 1971, and in no other year had more than 129).

In the American League (for Oakland, Baltimore, and
New York), Reggie Jackson had 100 or more
strikeouts 13 straight times (1968-80), plus five other
times, for a major league record of 18.

13.14 **B. Jimmy Foxx**   Playing for the Philadelphia Athletics
and Boston Red Sox, Foxx did it seven times:
1929-31, 1933, 1935-36, and 1941. Vince DiMaggio
holds the National League record of six times. Foxx's
totals were not that bad, though, by today's standards:
He topped 100 strikeouts only twice.

13.15 **A. Lou Brock**   Brock was caught 307 times.
Henderson, who finished the 1990 season only two
short of Brock's all-time stolen base total of 938, will
probably pass Brock in the caught-stealing category,
too, before his career is over. Official caught-stealing
records, however, date back only 46 years in the
National League and 70 years in the American
League. The SABR records committee, extrapolating
available caught-stealing data on Ty Cobb, estimate
that he was caught stealing at least 400 times.

13.16 **B. 20**   The Yankees did it against Boston on September
21, 1956, while losing a meaningless game (New
York had already clinched the pennant) by a score of
13-7. In the game, the Yankees left the bases loaded
three times. The National League record is 18, done
many times (the Cardinals did it the most of any
team, three times).

13.17 **A. Bob Feller**   Feller did it while pitching for
Cleveland in 1938. In the National League, Amos
Rusie holds the major league record, pitching for
New York; he walked 218 batters in 1893.

13.18 **A. Lefty Grove**   Grove whiffed 593 times in 1,369
at-bats. His lifetime average of .148 was extremely
low for a pitcher of his era, though he did hit 15
career home runs.

13.19 **C. Gene Mauch**   When he retired, Mauch had managed

more years—26 (from 1960-82 and 1985-87, for
Philadelphia, Montreal, Minnesota, and
California)—than anyone except Harris, Mack, and
McGraw. But unlike Mauch, the other three won
pennants.

13.20 **A. Dwight Gooden**   This tied the record for most
losses in an All-Star Game. Gooden has good
company, though. Other two-time All-Star losers
were Mort Cooper, Claude Passeau, Whitey Ford,
Luis Tiant, and Jim "Catfish" Hunter.

13.21 **B. Walter Johnson**   Johnson lost 65; of these, 26 were
by the score of 1-0, also a record. But he also *won* a
record number of complete game shutouts (110), and
3 non-complete shutouts.

13.22 **C. Brooks Robinson**   Robinson was on the losing side
15 times (and the nonwinning side 16 times, since he
played in one tie), as he happened to play in the
period from 1960-74, when the National League
dominated the contest.

13.23 **B. Chicago**   From 1901-89, Chicago lost 6,840 games.
The most wins in the league during this period—even
though the club did not join the league until
1903—are by New York, with 7,641.

13.24 **D. Philadelphia**   From 1883, when they entered the
league, through 1989, Philadelphia lost a total of
8,576 games. The team with the most wins from
1876-1989 was the Cubs, with 8,620 wins.

13.25 **C. Dave Stewart**   Pitching for Oakland, Stewart balked
16 times, or about once every 17 innings. Steve
Carlton holds the National League record of 11, set
while pitching for Philadelphia in 1979.

Chapter 14

By the Numbers

Asking someone to recall exactly how many times Bobby Bonds struck out in 1970 (189), or how many assists Bill Buckner had as a first baseman in 1971 (184), is not a very fair, or particularly interesting, question. But such numerical trivia can be turned into good quiz questions by offering a set of choices that are far enough apart to give the quiz taker a sporting chance to make a correct guess. That's the concept behind this chapter's quiz. (Answers and explanations begin on page 150.)

14.1 Babe Ruth had his famous total of 60 homers in 1927. What was his best home run total for a season prior to that year?
   A. 59
   B. 54
   C. 44
   D. 24

14.2 Since 1900, what is the most times a player has ever hit safely in a nine-inning game?
   A. 5
   B. 6
   C. 7
   D. 8

14.3 What is the most total bases a player has ever had in a
single game?
A. 16
B. 18
C. 20
D. 22

14.4 What was the top annual salary on the 1869 Cincinnati
Red Stockings?
A. $18
B. $180
C. $1,800
D. $18,000

14.5 In 1990, Jose Canseco of the A's signed a five-year
contract for how much, giving him the largest contract of
any player?
A. $13.5 million
B. $18.5 million
C. $23.5 million
D. $28.5 million

14.6 In 1944, Red Barrett of the Boston Braves set a record for
throwing the fewest pitches ever in a nine-inning
complete game. How many pitches did he throw?
A. 58
B. 68
C. 78
D. 88

14.7 In the 100-year period from 1891 through 1990, how
many seasons were there in which no major league
no-hitters were thrown?
A. 19
B. 39
C. 59
D. 79

14.8 What is the most major league no-hitters ever thrown in a single calendar month?
  A. 1
  B. 3
  C. 5
  D. 7

14.9 The 1982 All-Star balloting was higher than in any year. How many fan votes were cast that year?
  A. 1.5 million
  B. 3.1 million
  C. 9.3 million
  D. 18.6 million

14.10 What is the most innings an All-Star Game has ever gone, through 1990?
  A. 9
  B. 12
  C. 15
  D. 18

14.11 Through 1990, eight All-Star Games had gone into extra innings. How many of these did the National League win?
  A. 0
  B. 2
  C. 6
  D. 8

14.12 The American League set a major league record—and also an all-time sports record for any league—with its 1989 attendance. What was it, to the nearest million?
  A. 10 million
  B. 20 million
  C. 30 million
  D. 40 million

14.13 Ron Hunt set a record in 1971 for being hit by a pitch the most times in a single season. How many times did he do it that year?
  A. 10
  B. 30
  C. 50
  D. 70

14.14 In 1947, Roy Cullenbine set a major league record by drawing at least one walk in each of how many consecutive games?
A. 12
B. 22
C. 32
D. 42

14.15 What is the record for driving in at least one run in the most consecutive games?
A. 7
B. 12
C. 17
D. 22

14.16 What is the record for the most consecutive hits by a batter, with no walks intervening?
A. 6
B. 8
C. 10
D. 12

14.17 What is the most games a pitcher has ever appeared in in one season?
A. 66
B. 86
C. 106
D. 126

14.18 In 1988, Orel Hershiser set a record by pitching how many consecutive scoreless innings?
A. 29
B. 39
C. 49
D. 59

14.19 In his record sixth no-hitter (June 11, 1990, Texas over
Oakland 5-0), Nolan Ryan also struck out 14, extending
his record of being in double figures in strikeouts the
most times of any pitcher in history. Exactly how many
times had he done it before that no-hitter?
A. 100
B. 200
C. 300
D. 400

14.20 What is the modern record for the most runs ever scored
by a player in a single season?
A. 117
B. 147
C. 177
D. 207

14.21 What is the all-time record for triples in a season?
A. 18
B. 24
C. 30
D. 36

14.22 Catchers are not usually known for being fleet of foot.
What is the most bases a catcher has stolen in a single
season?
A. 12
B. 24
C. 36
D. 48

14.23 What is the *fewest* wins recorded during the regular
season by the winningest pitcher on a team that went on
to win the World Series?
A. 14
B. 16
C. 18
D. 20

14.24 World War II interrupted the careers of many players at their primes, such as Joe DiMaggio, Bob Feller, and Ted Williams. Of all servicemen who had ever played in the major leagues, how many were killed in action during that war?
  A. none
  B. 2
  C. 10
  D. 25

14.25 Which one of these totals is greater than 1?
  A. the number of home runs Babe Ruth lost from his career total because of an old rule that deprived a batter of credit for a home run if the would-be homer drove in the winning run ahead of the batter (in the bottom of the ninth or an extra inning)
  B. the number of home runs hit by Babe Ruth in the minor leagues
  C. the number of times Ruth hit three home runs in a regular-season game in the American League
  D. the number of World Series in which Ruth's slugging average was 1.000 or higher

Answers and Explanations

14.1 **A. 59**   He hit 59 in 1921; by hitting 60, he broke his own record for most home runs in a season. His other 50-plus seasons were 1920 and 1928, with 54 home runs in each.

14.2 **C. 7**   Rennie Stennett (Pittsburgh) went 7-for-7 on September 16, 1975 in a 22-0 wipeout of the Cubs. (He even went 2-for-2 in an inning—twice.) Seven hits equaled the feat of Wilbert Robinson, who did it for Baltimore in 1892.

14.3 **B. 18**   Joe Adcock hit four homers and a double on July 31, 1954, for the Milwaukee Braves, playing the Dodgers at Ebbets Field. The American League record is 16, shared by several players. First to do it was Ty Cobb with three homers, two singles, and a double against the St. Louis Browns on May 5, 1925.

14.4 **C. $1,800**   Manager and centerfielder Harry Wright and his brother, shortstop George Wright, each earned $1,800. The lowest salary was $600 for Dick Hurley, who was billed as a "substitute."

14.5 **C. $23.5 million**   In 1989, Canseco had also set a record by receiving the largest single-season raise in baseball history: a $1.2 million raise to a contract of $1.6 million, representing a 351 percent increase over his previous year's pay (see also question 6.9).

14.6 **A. 58**   Throwing an average of just slightly more than two pitches per batter, Barrett won the game 2-0 over the Cincinnati Reds on August 10, 1944.

14.7 **A. 19**   There was at least one no-hitter in 81 of the 100 seasons. The years in which there were none are 1894, 1895, 1896, 1913, 1921, 1927, 1928, 1930, 1932, 1933, 1936, 1939, 1942, 1943, 1949, 1959, 1982, 1985, and 1989.

14.8   **C.   5**   Five were thrown in June 1990—an amazingly high total: on June 2, by Randy Johnson of Seattle; on June 11, by Nolan Ryan of Texas; on June 29, by both Dave Stewart of Oakland and Fernando Valenzuela of the Dodgers; and on June 30, by Andy Hawkins of the New York Yankees (who lost the game). The two no-hitters in two different games on the same date was also a first, as were the three no-hitters in 48 hours.

The season record for most no-hitters was also broken in 1990, when Terry Mulholland of Philadelphia pitched the eighth one of the season on August 15. Dave Stieb of Toronto extended the record by throwing the ninth no-hitter of the season on September 2. Previously, besides the five in June, Mark Langston and Mike Witt had combined on one for California on April 11, and Melido Perez of the White Sox had thrown a five-inning one (shortened on account of rain) on July 12. The previous record of seven no-hitters in a season had been set in 1908 and 1917.

14.9   **C.   9.3 million**   By comparison, the 1990 total was just 6.9 million—still more than in any year since 1982.

14.10   **C.   15**   Tony Perez of Cincinnati won the 1967 All-Star Game with a home run in the 15th inning, giving the National League a 2-1 victory. The game is also noteworthy because a combined total of 30 batters struck out for the two teams.

14.11   **D.   8**   The most recent one was in 1987, when a 13th inning triple by Tim Raines was the deciding blow.

14.12   **C.   30 million**   To be exact, it was 29,849,262. American League attendance has exceeded National League attendance in recent years, of course, since the league has 14 teams to the National League's 12. (The National League, however, plans to expand to 14 teams in the 1990s.) The American League was likely to break its own record in 1990, but figures were not yet available when this book went to print.

14.13   **C. 50**   Hunt achieved the record while playing for
Montreal. Lifetime, he was hit by a pitch 243 times,
the National League record. Don Baylor (Baltimore,
Oakland, California, New York Yankees, Boston,
Minnesota, 1970-88) holds the career record of 267.

14.14   **B. 22**   He did it from July 2-22, while playing for
Detroit, and had 34 walks total during the streak. In
the National League, Jack Clark holds the record of
walking in 16 straight games (for St. Louis, from July
18 to August 10, 1987), with a total of 28 walks.

14.15   **C. 17**   Ray Grimes of the Cubs drove in runs in 17
consecutive games in 1922. The American League
record of 13 was set by Taft Wright of the White Sox
in 1941.

14.16   **D. 12**   Walt Dropo set the mark playing for Detroit on
July 14-15, 1952.

14.17   **C. 106**   Mike Marshall appeared in 106 games for Los
Angeles in 1974. In 1979, he also pitched in an
American League record 90 games for Minnesota.
Kent Tekulve's 94 appearances for Pittsburgh in 1979
are the next highest season total after Marshall's 106.

14.18   **D. 59**   Pitching for Los Angeles, he broke the record of
another Dodger, Don Drysdale, who had pitched 58
consecutive scoreless innings in 1968. Walter
Johnson set the American League record in 1913 with
a streak of 55 2/3 scoreless innings.

14.19   **B. 200**   The no-hitter was his 201st double-figure
strikeout game.

14.20   **C. 177**   Babe Ruth scored 177 runs for the New York
Yankees in 1921.

14.21   **D. 36**   Owen "Chief" Wilson hit the 36 triples for
Pittsburgh in 1912. His next best total was only 14
triples (in 1913), but he did have at least 12 triples
every year from 1909-1914.

14.22 **C. 36** John Wathan, playing for Kansas City in 1982, stole 36. The National League record of 25 was set by John Stearns (New York) in 1978.

14.23 **A. 14** In 1979, when the Pittsburgh Pirates won the World Series, their staff win leader was John Candelaria, with just 14. In the American League, the lowest total ever was 15, shared by Lefty Gomez and Red Ruffing of the 1941 Yankees.

14.24 **B. 2** Elmer Gedeon, an outfielder who had played in five games for Washington, was killed when his plane was shot down in France in 1944; and Harry O'Neill, who had played in one game for the Philadelphia Athletics, died at Iwo Jima in 1945. (Neither Gedeon nor O'Neill was on a major league roster when the war began.) In all, more than 100 major leaguers or former major leaguers served in the war.

14.25 **D. the number of the World Series in which Ruth's slugging average was 1.000 or higher** Ruth's World Series slugging average was 1.000 in 1923 and 1.375 in 1928.

Ruth lost credit for a home run because of the rule in choice A on July 8, 1918 (see the answer to question 3.20)—but he did get credit for a triple. Otherwise, his home run total would have been 715 instead of 714. Ruth hit just one minor league home run, on September 5, 1914, while pitching for the Baltimore Orioles and shutting out Toronto 9-0, and he hit three homers in a game just once in each league (though he also did it once in the World Series).

Chapter 15

Seventh-Inning Stretch

This quiz is intended as a break from the single-subject themes of many of the preceding chapters. In it, you'll find a potpourri of questions on everything from famous debuts to unfortunate endings. (Answers and explanations begin on page 160.)

15.1 Who was the first National League player to earn at least $100,000 in a season?
  A. Hank Aaron
  B. Hank Greenberg
  C. Sandy Koufax
  D. Willie Mays

15.2 Nap Lajoie is listed on many all-time All-Star teams—at what position?
  A. first base
  B. second base
  C. third base
  D. shortstop

15.3 With what invention are the names Candy Cummings and
Fred Goldsmith linked?
  A. baseball shoes
  B. batting helmets
  C. the curveball
  D. signs given by coaches to baserunners

15.4 For a time, two All-Star Games were held each year
instead of just one. When was this?
  A. 1939-42
  B. 1949-52
  C. 1959-62
  D. 1969-72

15.5 When Jackie Robinson debuted with the Brooklyn
Dodgers in 1947, he received a great deal of attention in
the press as the National League's first black player. How
did his batting debut go?
  A. He hit for the cycle in his first game.
  B. He hit safely in each of his first 20 games.
  C. He struck out twice in a row, then homered twice in a
       row, all in his first game.
  D. He went 0-for-20 in his first five games.

15.6 Who has the record for the most home runs in a season by
a catcher?
  A. Johnny Bench
  B. Yogi Berra
  C. Roy Campanella
  D. Carlton Fisk

15.7 What actor played both major league baseball and NBA
basketball?
  A. Chuck Connors
  B. Fred Dryer
  C. Charlton Heston
  D. Ken Howard

15.8 On three different occasions, Orlando Cepeda was traded "straight up" for a single player. Who was *not* one of these players?
A. Ted Abernathy
B. Denny McLain
C. Ray Sadecki
D. Joe Torre

15.9 Who is the only lefthanded pitcher in this century to win 30 or more games in a season?
A. Lefty Grove
B. Sandy Koufax
C. Eddie Plank
D. Warren Spahn

15.10 Which of these players had the most at-bats during his career?
A. Lou Gehrig
B. Mickey Mantle
C. Babe Ruth
D. Ted Williams

15.11 Who was the first New York Met to hit a home run?
A. Choo Choo Coleman
B. Gil Hodges
C. Willie Mays
D. Marv Throneberry

15.12 Babe Ruth was the first player to hit a home run in an All-Star Game. But who hit the next two All-Star home runs?
A. Frankie Frisch
B. Lou Gehrig
C. Joe Medwick
D. Babe Ruth

15.13 What pitcher had the most wins during the 1950s?
A. Bob Lemon
B. Robin Roberts
C. Warren Spahn
D. Early Wynn

15.14 In 1980, a new statistic was added: game-winning RBIs. What exactly is one?
   A. an RBI that breaks a tie in the bottom of the ninth or the bottom half of any extra inning
   B. the RBI that gives the team the run that is one more than the opposing team scores
   C. the RBI that gives the winning team the lead that it never relinquishes
   D. the RBI that puts a team ahead for good, but only if the game was tied—or the winning team was behind—at some point after the first five innings

15.15 What team did Hall of Fame pitcher Three Finger Brown help win four pennants and two World Championships?
   A. Chicago Cubs
   B. Chicago White Sox
   C. Philadelphia Athletics
   D. St. Louis Cardinals

15.16 In 1990, which brand of baseball cards issued a special nine-card Reggie Jackson set, including a limited number of cards autographed by Jackson?
   A. Donruss
   B. Score
   C. Topps
   D. Upper Deck

15.17 Who set a record by getting 25 pinch hits in a season?
   A. Smokey Burgess
   B. Vic Davalillo
   C. Jose Morales
   D. Rusty Staub

15.18 What is the record for the highest single-season batting average by a pinch-hitter, based on a minimum of 30 at-bats?
   A. .336
   B. .386
   C. .436
   D. .486

15.19   Before Babe Ruth became the major league lifetime
        home run leader, the record for career home runs was
        held by Roger Connor, who had played from 1880-97.
        How many home runs did Connor hit?
        A. 136
        B. 236
        C. 336
        D. 436

15.20   What team holds the record for the most losses in a single
        season since 1900?
        A. New York Mets
        B. Philadelphia Phillies
        C. Seattle Mariners
        D. Toronto Blue Jays

15.21   Who was the oldest pitcher ever to win 20 games in a
        season?
        A. Phil Niekro
        B. Gaylord Perry
        C. Warren Spahn
        D. Cy Young

15.22   How large are the coaches' boxes behind first and third
        base?
        A. 3 feet by 6 feet
        B. 6 feet by 12 feet
        C. 10 feet by 20 feet
        D. 15 feet by 30 feet

15.23   Who was the first pitcher to win three games in a single
        League Championship Series?
        A. Dennis Eckersley
        B. Bruce Kison
        C. Jesse Orosco
        D. Jim Palmer

15.24 Which of these uniform numbers has *not* been retired by
the New York Yankees?
   A. 1
   B. 2
   C. 3
   D. 4

15.25 From 1901-90, how many major league players were
fatally injured on the field?
   A. none
   B. 1
   C. 5
   D. 10

Answers and Explanations

15.1 **B. Hank Greenberg**   Pittsburgh paid Greenberg
$100,000 in 1947, his final season. Though he batted
only .249, he still hit 25 home runs and led the league
in walks (104) in just 125 games.

15.2 **B. second base**   In 21 seasons from 1896-1916, playing
for both leagues' Philadelphia clubs as well as
Cleveland, Lajoie wound up with 3,251 hits and a
lifetime batting average of .339. His best year was
1901, when he led the American League in batting
(.422), hits (229), doubles (48), home runs (14), RBIs
(125), and runs (145), according to *The Baseball
Encyclopedia*. According to *Total Baseball*, Lajoie hit
an even higher .426 that year.

15.3 **C. the curveball**   Cummings, a star National
Association pitcher from 1872-75, who also pitched
two years in the National League (1876-77), is
usually credited with the invention of the pitch, for
which he claimed to have gotten the idea in 1863. His
1908 article, "How I Pitched the First Curve,"
reinforced his claim. But Goldsmith is believed to
have been the first to have made a public
demonstration of the pitch, in 1870, and supposedly,
he became bitter at not having been recognized as the
inventor. Cummings, who was also the first major
leaguer to pitch two complete-game victories in one
day (for Hartford against Cincinnati on September 9,
1876), was elected to the Hall of Fame in 1939.

15.4 **C. 1959-62**   Each year, the first game was played in
early July, and the second in late July (except in
1959, when the second game was played on
August 3). During that period, the National League
won five games, the American League two, and there
was one tie—a game played in Fenway Park on July
31, 1961, which was called on account of rain after
nine innings with the score 1-1.

15.5 **D. He went 0-for-20 in his first five games.** But he was able to shrug off his poor start, and ended up with a .297 average for the year.

15.6 **C. Roy Campanella**   Campanella hit 40 home runs as a catcher for Brooklyn in 1953 and also had 1 as a pinch-hitter that year. Bench hit 45 home runs in 1970, but only 38 as a catcher (he hit 6 as an outfielder and 1 as a first baseman). Carlton Fisk holds the American League record with 33 in 1985; he also had 4 that year as a designated hitter.

15.7 **A. Chuck Connors**   Connors pinch hit once for Brooklyn in 1949, and played first base in 66 games for the Cubs in 1951, hitting .239 with 2 home runs. He also played 53 games for the Boston Celtics in the 1940s.

15.8 **A. Ted Abernathy**   Cepeda was traded from San Francisco to St. Louis in May 1966 for Sadecki; St. Louis traded him to Atlanta for Torre in March 1969; Atlanta traded him to Oakland for McLain in June 1972.

15.9 **A. Lefty Grove**   Grove won 31 in 1931 for the Philadelphia Athletics. (A look at the nineteenth century, however, shows that Lady Baldwin won 42 for Detroit in 1886, Matt Kilroy won 47 for Baltimore in 1887, and Frank Killen won 30 for Pittsburgh in 1896.)

15.10 **C. Babe Ruth**   Ruth had 8,399 at-bats. Mantle had 8,102, Gehrig had 8,001, and Williams, whose career was interrupted by both World War II and the Korean War, had 7,706.

15.11 **B. Gil Hodges**   Hodges homered on April 11, 1962, at St. Louis. Though New York finished in last place that year, a distant 60 1/2 games out of first, their 139 home runs ranked sixth out of the 10 teams in the league.

15.12   **A.   Frankie Frisch**   In the first All-Star Game (July 6, 1933), Ruth homered for the American League in the third inning and Frisch homered for the National League in the sixth. Frisch homered again in the first inning of the second All-Star Game (July 10, 1934). A switch hitter, he connected off righthander Al Crowder and Lefty Gomez. Both of his home runs were in losing causes, as the Junior Circuit won the first game 4-2 and the second 9-7. In regular season play, Frisch had a modest 105 lifetime home runs, and never more than 12 in one year.

15.13   **C.   Warren Spahn**   Spahn won 202—the only time a pitcher has won 200 games in a calendar decade since Walter Johnson and Grover Cleveland Alexander did it from 1910-19. Next best in the 1950s were Roberts with 199, Wynn with 188, Billy Pierce with 155, and Lemon with 150.

15.14   **C.   the RBI that gives the winning team the lead that it never relinquishes**   The statistic, which seemed to have almost as much to do with luck as with skill, was abandoned after 1988. Keith Hernandez ended up as the all-time leader in the category, with 129 from 1980-88 for St. Louis and the New York Mets. Eddie Murray of Baltimore had 117, the most in the American League.

15.15   **A.   Chicago Cubs**   With Brown as the ace of their staff, the Cubs won pennants in 1906-08 and 1910, and won the World Series in 1907 and 1908. Brown had lost most of his forefinger and his middle finger was mangled in an acorn grinder at age seven. Despite this handicap, he won 20 games for Chicago for six straight years (1906-11), with at least 25 wins four of those years. He ended his 14-year career in 1916 with a record of 239-129, as well as 48 saves and a World Series record of 5-4. His career ERA of 2.06 ranks third on the all-time list behind Ed Walsh (1.82, pitching for the White Sox and Braves from 1904-17) and Addie Joss (1.88, pitching for Cleveland from 1902-10).

15.16 **D. Upper Deck**   Jackson autographed 2,500 copies of
the ninth card in the set.

15.17 **C. Jose Morales**   Morales did it for Montreal in 1976,
in 78 at-bats (a .321 average). Manny Mota holds the
career record of 150 pinch-hits (1962-80 and 1982),
playing for San Francisco, Pittsburgh, Montreal, and
Los Angeles.

15.18 **D. .486**   Ed Kranepool went 17-for-35 as pinch-hitter
for the Mets in 1974. His lifetime average as a
pinch-hitter was .277. (The record lifetime average
for a pinch-hitter, based on at least 150 at-bats, is
Tommy Davis's .320, playing from 1959-76 for Los
Angeles, the Mets, the White Sox, Houston, Oakland,
the Cubs, Baltimore, California, and Kansas City.)

15.19 **A. 136**   Ruth broke Connor's record in 1921, when he
hit his 137th home run. Connor played for the
National League's Troy, New York, Philadelphia, and
St. Louis clubs, as well as a year for New York in the
Players' League. Connor ranks fifth all-time in
triples, with 233.

15.20 **A. New York Mets**   In 1962, their first season, the
Mets were a woeful 40-120. The Philadelphia
Athletics set the American League record of 117
losses in 1916 (they won 36). In 1899 the Cleveland
National League team won 20 and lost 134.

15.21 **C. Warren Spahn**   Spahn turned 42 on April 23, 1963,
and went on to a record of 23-7 that year for
Milwaukee. Cy Young was the oldest American
Leaguer to win 20, with a 21-11 season for Boston in
1908 at age 41.

15.22 **C. 10 feet by 20 feet**   Also, they are located 15 feet
from the bases.

15.23 **C. Jesse Orosco**   Orosco won three LCS games, all in
relief, in 1986, pitching for the Mets as they defeated
the Astros four games to two. (He also got two saves

in the World Series that year.) For Oakland in 1988, Eckersley saved four games in a four-game series—one record that's certain never to be broken. Kison, pitching for Pittsburgh in 1971-72 and 1974-75, complied an LCS record of 4-0, giving him the most wins for an undefeated LCS pitcher. Palmer, too, has a notable LCS accomplishment, with four consecutive complete game victories for Baltimore (once each in 1969-71 and 1973).

15.24 **B.** **2** Billy Martin's number 1 was retired in 1986; Babe Ruth's 3 was retired in 1948; Lou Gehrig's 4 was retired in 1939. Gehrig was the first player on any team to have his number retired.

15.25 **B.** **1** On August 16, 1920, Ray Chapman of the Cleveland Indians, a shortstop with a career batting average of .278 in nine seasons, was hit in the head by a pitch thrown by Carl Mays of the Yankees. His skull fractured, Chapman died the next day. (Not until many years later did batting helmets become standard equipment.) Mays, a fine pitcher, managed to keep pitching well despite the tragedy, finishing 26-11 in 1920 and 27-9 in 1921. His career record was 208-126, with an ERA of 2.92.

Chapter 16

They Also Play the Game

Major league baseball may be the highest level of the game, but there's a huge system of minor leagues, colleges, and competition for youngsters at many different age levels—as well as professional leagues in other countries. These other arenas have produced many major league players, as well as some remarkable records. (Answers and explanations begin on page 170.)

16.1 To be eligible to play in Little League, how old must a boy or girl be on August 1 of the calendar year in which the games are played?
A. at least 7, at most 11
B. at least 8, at most 12
C. at least 9, at most 13
D. at least 10, at most 14

16.2 In Little League, what is the distance from home to first base?
A. 45 feet
B. 60 feet
C. 75 feet
D. 90 feet

16.3 How long is a normal Little League game—that is, one
that is not cut short because of rain or darkness and does
not go into extra innings?
A. 5 innings
B. 6 innings
C. 7 innings
D. 9 innings

16.4 How many children play Little League in the U.S. each
year?
A. 25,000
B. 250,000
C. 2,500,000
D. 25,000,000

16.5 In 1974, the Little League charter was revised to allow
girls to play. Today, for each girl in Little League, about
how many boys are there?
A. 3.6
B. 36
C. 360
D. 3,600

16.6 Where is the Little League World Series played?
A. Fort Lauderdale, Florida
B. Gary, Indiana
C. Santa Barbara, California
D. Williamsport, Pennsylvania

16.7 Where is the College World Series played?
A. Cooperstown, New York
B. Omaha, Nebraska
C. Wichita, Kansas
D. It changes every year.

16.8 What format is followed in the College World Series?
A. single elimination
B. double elimination
C. round robin
D. best of seven

16.9 Roger Clemens, Greg Swindell, Calvin Shiraldi, and
Bruce Ruffin all pitched for what college team when it
won the College World Series in 1983?
A. Arizona
B. Michigan
C. Texas
D. USC

16.10 Who, pitching for Yale against St. John's in an NCAA
playoff game, pitched an 11-inning no-hitter—the longest
in NCAA history—only to lose in the 12th inning 1-0?
A. Ron Darling
B. Bret Saberhagen
C. John Tudor
D. Frank Viola

16.11 Who, in 13 full seasons in the Negro Leagues, won four
batting titles and nine home run crowns, and ended up
with a record lifetime average of .384?
A. Oscar Charleston
B. Ray Dandridge
C. Josh Gibson
D. Buck Leonard

16.12 A dealer in memorabilia was indicted in the 1980s for
stealing $300,000 worth of bats, autographed balls,
posters, and other items from what star of the St. Louis
Stars of the National Negro Baseball League?
A. James "Cool Papa" Bell
B. Ray Dandridge
C. Martin DiHigo
D. Monte Irvin

16.13 What citizen of Taiwan, playing Japanese baseball, hit
more home runs than Hank Aaron?
A. Hiromitsu Ochiai
B. Sadaharu Oh
C. Shigeo Nagashima
D. Terushi Nakajima

16.14 Many American players have played for Japanese teams
in recent years. But how many foreign players, whether
from the U.S. or anywhere else, may a Japanese team
have on its roster at one time?
A. 2
B. 5
C. 12
D. There is no limit.

16.15 What is the oldest minor league?
A. American Association
B. International League
C. Pacific Coast League
D. Texas League

16.16 What is the minor league record for most lifetime hits?
A. between 1,000 and 2,000
B. between 2,000 and 3,000
C. between 3,000 and 4,000
D. more than 4,000

16.17 What is the minor league record for the most home runs
in a career?
A. 184
B. 284
C. 484
D. 884

16.18 What is the minor league record for the most home runs
in a season?
A. 42
B. 57
C. 72
D. 87

16.19 What is the minor league record for most home runs hit
by one player in a game?
A. 2
B. 4
C. 6
D. 8

16.20 What is the minor league record for most career wins by a pitcher?
A. 83
B. 183
C. 283
D. 383

16.21 Joe DiMaggio's 56-game consecutive hitting streak is well-known. But what was DiMaggio's longest consecutive game hitting streak in the *minor* leagues?
A. He never played in the minors.
B. 21
C. 41
D. 61

16.22 What is the minor league record for the most RBIs in a season?
A. 104
B. 154
C. 204
D. 254

16.23 A minor league attendance record was set in 1982 in an American Association game between Denver and Omaha. How many attended that game?
A. 20,666
B. 35,666
C. 50,666
D. 65,666

16.24 What is the most innings a minor league game has ever gone?
A. 18
B. 23
C. 28
D. 33

16.25 What are the minimum age requirements for the recently formed Senior Professional Baseball Association?
A. 32 for catchers, 34 for noncatchers
B. 35 for all players
C. 38 for catchers, 40 for noncatchers
D. 43 for catchers, 45 for noncatchers

Answers and Explanations

16.1 **C. at least 9, at most 13**   Children 6-8 play in
"tee-ball" leagues, in which the ball is teed up instead
of pitched. (Eight- to 12-year-olds may also play on
minor league Little League teams.) There are also
Senior League teams for 13- to 15-year-olds, with a
Junior League division just for 13-year-olds. Players
16-18 can play in Big Leagues.

16.2 **B. 60 feet**   Also, the distance from home to the pitching
rubber is 46 feet, and the mound is 6 inches high.

16.3 **B. 6 innings**   If the game is shortened on account of
weather or darkness, it must have gone four innings
for the result to count.

16.4 **C. 2,500,000**   In addition, more than 450,000 older
children play in Babe Ruth leagues.

16.5 **C. 360**   In all, about 7,000 of the 2.5 million Little
League players are girls.

16.6 **D. Williamsport, Pennsylvania**   Since its inception in
1947, it has been played in Williamsport, which is
where the Little League was founded in 1939.
Through 1990, teams from Taiwan have won the
Series 14 times (last in 1990); the U.S. states that
have sent the most winning teams are Connecticut
and Pennsylvania (four each).

   Gary and Fort Lauderdale have been sites of
similar competitions for the older Senior League
(13-15) and Big League (16-18) players.

16.7 **B. Omaha, Nebraska**   It moved from Wichita to
Omaha in 1950, and has been played there ever since,
before steadily increasing crowds.

16.8 **B. double elimination**   Eight teams compete over a
nine-day period in June.

16.9   **C.   Texas**   Texas had won before, in 1949, 1950, and 1975. The team that has won the most NCAA championships is USC, with 11 wins, including a record five wins in a row from 1970-74.

16.10   **A.   Ron Darling**   Viola was the opposing pitcher. Darling and Viola became teammates when Viola joined the Mets in 1989.

16.11   **C.   Josh Gibson**   Named to the Hall of Fame in 1972, Gibson is considered one of the Negro Leagues' greatest catchers, and perhaps their greatest player. In 1943, he was diagnosed as having a brain tumor, but he continued to play, winning three home run titles the next three years. He died suddenly of a stroke in 1947, at the age of 35. Charleston, Dandridge, and Leonard are other Negro League players who have been elected to the Hall of Fame.

16.12   **A.   James "Cool Papa" Bell**   Bell played for the Stars (and a few other teams) from 1922-50, batting over .400 a number of times. An outfielder, he was best-known for his great speed and base-stealing ability.

16.13   **B.   Sadaharu Oh**   He hit 868 home runs. His average of one home run per 10.65 at-bats compares favorably with Babe Ruth's ratio of 1 home run per 11.76 at-bats, and very favorably with Aaron's 1 per 16.37 at-bats.

16.14   **A.   2**   Most come from the United States or Taiwan.

16.15   **B.   International League**   The International League was founded as the Eastern League in 1884, and became the International League for the first time in 1886. Babe Ruth, pitching for the league's Providence club in 1914, shut out Toronto on one hit and hit his only minor league home run. Lefty Grove anchored the Baltimore pitching staff from 1920-24, when the Orioles were one of the greatest minor league teams ever. Before being called up to the

majors, Jackie Robinson played for the league's
Montreal franchise in 1946.

16.16 **C. between 3,000 and 4,000** Spencer Harris had 3,617
hits as a minor league outfielder from 1921-48, and
also set career records for runs (2,287) and total bases
(5,434). He played only briefly in the American
League in 1925-26 and 1929-30 for Chicago,
Washington, and Philadelphia, batting .249 (94 hits in
377 at-bats).

16.17 **C. 484** Hector Espino hit them playing as a first
baseman and outfielder in the Mexican Leagues from
1960-84. After a brief stint in the International
League in 1964, he said he never again wanted to
play in the United States on account of racial
discrimination—and he never did.

16.18 **C. 72** Joe Bauman, a 6' 5", 235 pound Oklahoman, hit
them for the Roswell Rockets of the Longhorn
League in 1954. He also had 224 RBIs and a .400
batting average that year, as a 32-year old first
baseman. Bauman never made it to the majors.

16.19 **D. 8** Nig Clarke, playing for Corsicana in the Texas
League, hit eight home runs in eight at-bats on June
15, 1902, when a Sunday game was played in a
short-fenced park in Ennis, Texas, to circumvent blue
laws. His team won 51-3 over Texarkana.

16.20 **D. 383** Bill Thomas, who never pitched in the majors,
is the record holder. He might have won many more,
but an Evangeline League betting scandal kept him
out of action for nearly three years in 1947-49.

16.21 **D. 61** DiMaggio hit in 61 straight while playing for the
San Francisco Seals in 1933 when he was only 18.
But the all-time minor league consecutive game
hitting streak belongs to Joe Wilhoit, who hit in 69
straight for Wichita in the Western League in 1919.
Wilhoit had played in the majors from 1916-18, and

played briefly with the Red Sox after his great streak, during which he batted an amazing .505.

16.22 **D.** **254** Bob Crues got them playing for Amarillo in the West Texas-New Mexico League in 1948. The same year, he batted .404 and hit 69 home runs, a record eight of them coming with the bases loaded. He never made it to the major leagues, though.

16.23 **D.** **65,666** In cities without major league teams, minor league baseball is sometimes a big draw, and the focus of newspaper sports pages all summer. In 1983, the Louisville Redbirds became the first minor league team to draw over 1,000,000 fans in one season. (Note: The minor league American Association is not connected with the major league of the same name that existed from 1882-91.)

16.24 **D.** **33** The game, played in 1981 between the Pawtucket Red Sox and the Rochester Red Wings, was suspended after 32 innings, at 4:07 Easter Sunday morning. The game was won by Pawtucket 3-2 in the 33rd when play resumed June 23. The winning pitcher was Bob Ojeda, one of whose teammates was Wade Boggs. One of the players on the losing side was Cal Ripken Jr.

16.25 **A.** **32 for catchers, 34 for noncatchers** In August, 1990, the winter league decided to reduce its minimum age from 35 to 34 for noncatchers, while leaving it at 32 for catchers. At the same time, the league announced other changes: Four of its original eight Florida teams folded (Orlando, Pompano Beach-Miami, St. Lucie, and Winter Haven); another Florida team moved from Bradenton to Daytona Beach; franchises in Fort Myers, St. Petersburg, and West Palm Beach remained in place; and new teams were added in San Bernadino, California and Sun City, Arizona. The league also reduced its schedule, which runs from late November to early February, from 72 games to 56.

Chapter 17

On the Screen and Between the Covers

Both baseball and movies developed into important parts of American culture at about the same time—which may be one reason that Hollywood has made so many baseball films, both fact and fiction. The game also pops up frequently in other media, such as television and books. This quiz tests how much attention you've been paying to these off-the-field contributors to baseball lore. (Answers and explanations begin on page 179.)

17.1 What movie was based on W.P. Kinsella's book *Shoeless Joe*?

    A. *Bang the Drum Slowly*
    B. *Field of Dreams*
    C. *The Kid from Cleveland*
    D. *Safe at Home*

17.2 Who portrayed pitching great Grover Cleveland Alexander in the 1952 film *The Winning Team*?

    A. Montgomery Clift
    B. Burt Lancaster
    C. Ray Milland
    D. Ronald Reagan

17.3 When did the poem "Casey at the Bat" first appear in print?
   A. 1858
   B. 1888
   C. 1918
   D. 1948

17.4 Who played the Devil's temptress Lola in the 1958 film *Damn Yankees* ?
   A. Doris Day
   B. Lee Remick
   C. Elizabeth Taylor
   D. Gwen Verdon

17.5 What is the title of political columnist George Will's 1990 book on baseball?
   A. *Ball Four*
   B. *Men at Play*
   C. *Men at Work*
   D. *Strike Three*

17.6 Which TV sitcom does *not* feature a leading character who supposedly is or was a major league baseball player?
   A. *The Bad News Bears*
   B. *Ball Four*
   C. *Cheers*
   D. *Who's the Boss?*

17.7 What player was the subject of the 1957 film *Fear Strikes Out*?
   A. Johnny Fear
   B. Jackie Jensen
   C. Jumpy Joiner
   D. Jimmy Piersall

17.8 What player portrayed himself in the main role in one of these movies?
   A. Dizzy Dean in *The Pride of St. Louis*
   B. Lou Gehrig in *Pride of the Yankees*
   C. Jackie Robinson in *The Jackie Robinson Story*
   D. Babe Ruth in *The Babe Ruth Story*

17.9 In what movie does chemistry professor Vernon Simpson
accidentally discover a substance that repels wood—and
then use it to become a pitching sensation?
A. *The Absent-Minded Professor*
B. *It Happens Every Spring*
C. *The Secret of My Success*
D. *Wood-n't You Know?*

17.10 Roger Kahn's 1972 best-seller *The Boys of Summer* is an
account of a chapter in the history of what team?
A. Boston Red Sox
B. Brooklyn Dodgers
C. Chicago Cubs
D. New York Yankees

17.11 Whose autobiography is titled *Me and the Spitter*?
A. Don Drysdale
B. Tommy John
C. Gaylord Perry
D. Rube Waddell

17.12 What player was the subject of the 1974 TV movie *It's
Good to be Alive* ?
A. Jim Abbott
B. Roy Campanella
C. Pete Gray
D. Dummy Taylor

17.13 A 1983 TV series starring Michael Nouri was centered on
a fictitious minor league team. What was the name of the
team?
A. Bay City Bluebirds
B. Canal City Crocodiles
C. Canyon City Coyotes
D. Desert City Dogs

17.14 What is the name of the magazine subtitled "The Official
Magazine of the Major League Baseball Players Alumni
Association"?
A. *The Good Old Days*
B. *Old Times*
C. *The Show*
D. *Vet Views*

17.15 Who wrote the 1952 novel *The Natural*, on which the
1984 film starring Robert Redford was based?
  A. Ernest Hemingway
  B. Harper Lee
  C. Bernard Malamud
  D. William Styron

17.16 Who wrote the best-selling book *Baseball Is a Funny
Game*?
  A. Jim Bouton
  B. Sidd Finch
  C. Joe Garagiola
  D. Bob Uecker

17.17 In how many of the *Bad News Bears* movies did Walter
Matthau play the team's coach?
  A. 0
  B. 1
  C. 2
  D. 3

17.18 In the 1951 comedy *Angels in the Outfield*, what team
receives divine assistance?
  A. Chicago Cubs
  B. Pittsburgh Pirates
  C. St. Louis Browns
  D. Washington Senators

17.19 What character was played by Bob Uecker on the
late-'80s TV sitcom *Mr. Belvedere*?
  A. Mr. Belvedere
  B. George Owens
  C. Kevin Owens
  D. Wesley Owens

17.20 What player, whose jet once crash-landed in Korea
during the Korean War, wrote an autobiography titled *My
Turn at Bat* ?
  A. Lou Boudreau
  B. Jackie Jensen
  C. Harvey Kuenn
  D. Ted Williams

17.21 Johnny Berardino, who played all four infield positions and hit a lifetime .249 for the Browns, Cleveland, and Pittsburgh from 1939-42 and 1946-52, is known to soap opera fans as a long-time star of what series?
   A. *As the World Turns*
   B. *Days of Our Lives*
   C. *General Hospital*
   D. *Ryan's Hope*

17.22 Who played Monty Stratton, the White Sox pitcher who lost a leg in an off-season hunting accident in 1938, in the 1949 movie *The Stratton Story*?
   A. Gary Cooper
   B. Errol Flynn
   C. James Stewart
   D. John Wayne

17.23 In the TV series *Father Dowling Mysteries*, which team's emblem is seen on Father Dowling's jacket in the opening credit sequence?
   A. California Angels
   B. Chicago Cubs
   C. Chicago White Sox
   D. Los Angeles Dodgers

17.24 What was the title of journalist Robert Whiting's book about Japanese baseball?
   A. *Dragons of the Diamond*
   B. *Samurai Sluggers*
   C. *You Gotta Have Wa*
   D. *Zen and the Art of Fielding*

17.25 What is the name of the second baseman in the classic Abbott & Costello comedy routine "Who's on First?"
   A. I Don't Give a Darn
   B. I Don't Know
   C. Tomorrow
   D. True

Answers and Explanations

17.1 **B.** *Field of Dreams* The book is about Shoeless Joe Jackson, owner of the third highest lifetime batting average in history, who was banned from baseball by Commissioner Kenesaw Mountain Landis after the 1919 Black Sox scandal in which some White Sox players allegedly threw the series to the Cincinnati Reds.

17.2 **D. Ronald Reagan** The film is fairly good, although it follows the predictable Hollywood formula that was standard in those days. Doris Day co-stars as his wife.

17.3 **B. 1888** It appeared in the San Francisco *Examiner* on June 3, 1888. Ernest Thayer, who was writing a humor column for the paper at the time, is now well-established to have been the author, although certain poetry books have attributed it to others.

17.4 **D. Gwen Verdon** Ray Walston played the Devil, and Tab Hunter starred as a rejuvenated star player. The film was based on the Broadway musical of the same title, featuring such songs as "Whatever Lola Wants" and "You Gotta Have Heart." Remick played Lola in a later TV version of the play.

17.5 **C.** *Men at Work* The book is subtitled "The Craft of Baseball."

17.6 **A.** *The Bad News Bears* The little league team's coach in the show, Morris Buttermaker (played by Jack Warden), is supposed to have been a former *minor* league player. The series ran from 1979-80. *Ball Four,* an even shorter-lived series of 1976, was set in a major league locker room. Jim Barton, played by real-life former major leaguer Jim Bouton, and several other characters were all supposed to be major leaguers. In the long-running *Cheers* (1982-present), bartender and sometimes bar-owner

Sam Malone (played by Ted Danson) is supposed to have been a former Red Sox pitcher. On *Who's the Boss?* (1984-present), housekeeper Tony Micelli (played by Tony Danza) is also supposed to be a retired major league ballplayer.

17.7 **D. Jimmy Piersall**   Anthony Perkins played the outfielder/shortstop, who had a lifetime batting average of .272 in 17 years (1950, 1952-1967) for the Boston Red Sox, Cleveland, Washington, the New York Mets, and the Los Angeles-California Angels. The film was based on Piersall's book of the same title, which recounted his own struggles to overcome a nervous breakdown during the 1952 season. Piersall went on to win two Gold Gloves and have his best season at the plate in 1961, when he batted .322 for Cleveland.

17.8 **C. Jackie Robinson in *The Jackie Robinson Story*** Robinson played himself in this 1950 film. Dan Dailey played Dizzy Dean in the 1952 film, in which Richard Crenna played Dizzy's brother Paul. Gary Cooper portrayed Lou Gehrig in the 1942 film, in which Babe Ruth did appear as himself (as did other Yankees Bill Dickey, Mark Koenig, and Bob Meusel). In *The Babe Ruth Story* (1948), which opened just three weeks before Ruth's death, Ruth was portrayed by William Bendix, who is better known for the radio and TV series *The Life of Riley*.

17.9 **B. *It Happens Every Spring***   Ray Milland played the pitcher/professor in this entertaining 1949 film. Things get tough when he starts to run low on his supply of the chemical at World Series time.

17.10 **B. Brooklyn Dodgers**   The book is about the great Brooklyn Dodger teams of the 1950s. Kahn was also a writer for for *The New York Herald Tribune*, *Newsweek*, and *Sports Illustrated*.

17.11 **C. Gaylord Perry**   Perry was accused of throwing spitballs throughout his career. Umpires would frequently search him for foreign substances he could be adding to the ball, but could never get the goods on him.

17.12 **B. Roy Campanella**   Paul Winfield portrayed Hall of Famer Campanella, who had a career-ending auto accident in 1958 that left him paralyzed. The other three choices are players who overcame serious handicaps. Abbott, who was born without a right hand, starred as a pitcher for the University of Michigan and went on directly to the California Angels in 1989. Gray, who lost his right arm as a child in a truck accident, played 77 games for the St. Louis Browns in 1945. (He hit only .218, but had had a sensational year for Memphis in the Southern Association in 1944, batting .333, stealing 68 bases, and winning the league's MVP award.) Taylor, a deaf-mute, pitched for Cleveland and the Giants from 1900-08, compiling a record of 115-106 (including 21 wins in 1904), with a 2.75 ERA.

17.13 **A. Bay City Bluebirds**   The name of the series was *The Bay City Blues*; it was produced by the same people who were responsible for the successful police drama *Hill Street Blues*. Nouri played Joe Rohner, the team's coach.

17.14 **C. *The Show***   Begun in June, 1990, it's a monthly magazine containing both human-interest and other baseball articles about both past and present players, managers, and other personnel.

17.15 **C. Bernard Malamud**   Malamud is also known for such other novels as *The Fixer*, for which he won the Pulitzer Prize for fiction in 1967, as well as for a number of short stories.

17.16 **C. Joe Garagiola**   Garagiola also replaced Mel Allen on Yankee broadcasts in 1965, and became a host on *The Today Show* in 1969-73.

17.17 **B. 1**   Matthau appeared only in the original film, *The*

Bad News Bears (1976), playing the team's coach.
There were two sequels—*The Bad News Bears in
Breaking Training* (1977) and *The Bad News Bears
Go to Japan* (1978)—neither of which pleased the
critics, many of whom had liked the original.

17.18 **B. Pittsburgh Pirates**   The film stars Paul Douglas,
Janet Leigh, Keenan Wynn, and Donna Corcoran.

17.19 **B. George Owens**   Besides playing George Owens
(Kevin and Wesley are George's sons), Uecker is also
known to TV viewers for appearing on beer
commercials and talk shows. Uecker appeared in 297
games from 1962-67 as a catcher and pinch-hitter for
the Braves, Cardinals, and Phillies. His lifetime
average was a meager .200.
   Mr. Belvedere, the sitcom family's British
housekeeper, was played by Christopher Hewett.

17.20 **D. Ted Williams**   After serving in World War II as a
flight instructor, Williams flew combat missions as a
pilot in Korea.

17.21 **C. *General Hospital***   He began playing Dr. Steve
Hardy when the show started in 1963 (though he used
the slightly shorter "Beradino" as his stage name).
Previously, he had played Sergeant Vince Cavelli in
the 1961-62 TV police series *The New Breed*.

17.22 **C. James Stewart**   Prior to his accident, Stratton
pitched in the major leagues from 1934-38. He was
an All-Star in 1937, when he wound up with a record
of 15-5 and a 2.40 ERA. After losing his leg, he never
pitched in the majors again—but he did prove he
could still pitch, posting a remarkable 18-8 record in
the East Texas League in 1946.

17.23 **B. Chicago Cubs**   The series is set in Chicago. Father
Dowling is played by Tom Bosley.

17.24 **C. *You Gotta Have Wa***   "Wa" has several meanings in
Japanese, but in this context it refers to "harmony."

Japanese baseball players are sometimes said to place greater emphasis on developing and maintaining perfect form and style than on winning.

17.25   **D. True**   The second baseman's name *is* "What"—just as the quiz question, which is actually a statement, says (go back and reread the "question" carefully).

Okay, it's a very unfair trick question…so maybe it will be fun to try it on someone else.

Chapter 18

It's a Team Game

Individual statistics may be the most memorable, but baseball is, after all, a team game. Teams have won the pennant, even the World Series, without a single 20-game winner and without any .300 hitters. Questions in this quiz cover both team accomplishments and the accomplishments of individual players for particular teams. (Answers and explanations begin on page 189.)

18.1 How many seasons did the Pilots play in Seattle?
    A. 1
    B. 3
    C. 5
    D. 7

18.2 What National League club has been the longest to play continuously in one city?
    A. Chicago
    B. Cincinnati
    C. Philadelphia
    D. St. Louis

18.3 In what year did a team first put its players' names on the backs of their uniforms?
    A. 1900
    B. 1920
    C. 1940
    D. 1960

18.4 What is the modern record for highest batting average by a team?

    A. .279

    B. .299

    C. .319

    D. .339

18.5 What is the most consecutive games a team has played without being shut out?

    A. 68

    B. 148

    C. 228

    D. 308

18.6 Which National League team's uniform shows a bat?

    A. Atlanta Braves

    B. Houston Astros

    C. Los Angeles Dodgers

    D. St. Louis Cardinals

18.7 What team holds the National League record for winning the most *consecutive* pennants?

    A. Cardinals

    B. Dodgers

    C. Giants

    D. Reds

18.8 What team holds the National League record for winning the most pennants?

    A. Cardinals

    B. Dodgers

    C. Giants

    D. Reds

18.9 The New York Yankees hold the record for winning the most pennants in major league baseball history. How many have they won?

    A. 13

    B. 23

    C. 33

    D. 43

18.10 In what decade did the Yankees win their most pennants?
   A. 1920s
   B. 1930s
   C. 1940s
   D. 1950s

18.11 What is the most home runs a single team has ever hit in one game?
   A. 6
   B. 8
   C. 10
   D. 12

18.12 According to management professor Gerald Scully's *The Business of Major League Baseball*, what team was the top moneymaker of the 1980s?
   A. Los Angeles Dodgers
   B. New York Mets
   C. New York Yankees
   D. San Francisco Giants

18.13 Who played more games for the Detroit Tigers during his career than anyone else?
   A. Ty Cobb
   B. Sam Crawford
   C. Charlie Gehringer
   D. Al Kaline

18.14 Who is the all-time Pirate leader in both home runs and RBIs?
   A. Hank Greenberg
   B. Ralph Kiner
   C. Willie Stargell
   D. Paul Waner

18.15 Although he did not play his entire career for the Yankees, Babe Ruth is the all-time Yankee leader in many offensive categories. In which of the following categories did Lou Gehrig overtake Ruth as Yankee leader?
   A. batting average
   B. extra-base hits
   C. runs
   D. total bases

18.16 What pitcher is the all-time Dodger team leader in wins?
  A. Don Drysdale
  B. Sandy Koufax
  C. Don Newcombe
  D. Don Sutton

18.17 At the beginning of the 1990 season, what active manager had been with his team the longest?
  A. Sparky Anderson
  B. Whitey Herzog
  C. Tony La Russa
  D. Tommy Lasorda

18.18 Of the famed Chicago Cubs double play combination "Tinker to Evers to Chance," who later managed the Cubs?
  A. Frank Chance
  B. Johnny Evers
  C. Joe Tinker
  D. all three

18.19 What team had the first all-switch-hitting infield?
  A. 1955 Red Sox
  B. 1965 Dodgers
  C. 1975 Reds
  D. 1985 Cardinals

18.20 What is the record for most stolen bases by one team in a season?
  A. 147
  B. 247
  C. 347
  D. 447

18.21 Which National League uniform does *not* have pinstripes?
  A. Chicago Cubs
  B. Los Angeles Dodgers
  C. New York Mets
  D. San Diego Padres

18.22 Who holds the Cincinnati record for the most career
home runs?
A. Johnny Bench
B. Ted Kluszewski
C. Joe Morgan
D. Frank Robinson

18.23 Who holds the Boston Red Sox record for the most home
runs in a single season?
A. Jimmy Foxx
B. Jim Rice
C. Ted Williams
D. Carl Yastrzemski

18.24 Who holds the Phillies career record for pitching in the
most games?
A. Grover Cleveland Alexander
B. Steve Carlton
C. Robin Roberts
D. Kent Tekulve

18.25 Which one of these statements is false?
A. George Foster played more years for Cincinnati than
for the New York Mets.
B. Joe Morgan played more years for Cincinnati than for
Houston.
C. Pete Rose played more years for Cincinnati than for
Philadelphia.
D. Frank Robinson played more years for Cincinnati
than for Baltimore.

Answers and Explanations

18.1 **A. 1**   After just one season, the expansion Pilots moved to Milwaukee in 1970 and became the Brewers. Several years later, Seattle completed the Kingdome and was awarded a new American League franchise, the Mariners, in 1977.

18.2 **A. Chicago**   The Cubs have been in the National League since it started in 1876. The franchise that is now the Atlanta Braves has also been in continuous existence since 1876, but has moved twice. Cincinnati was around in 1876, too, but dropped out of the league for a while (see question 2.24).

18.3 **D. 1960**   Chicago White Sox owner Bill Veeck was the first to do it. This later resulted in a trivia question: "What White Sox player carries his birthday on the back of his uniform?" The answer was Carlos May, with May 17.

18.4 **C. .319**   The New York Giants hit a record .319 in 1930, bolstered by Bill Terry's .401 average and Freddie Lindstrom's .379. The American League record of .316 is held by Detroit's 1921 club, with Harry Heilmann batting .394, and Ty Cobb .389.

18.5 **D. 308**   The New York Yankees went 308 games, from August 3, 1931 through August 2, 1933, without being shut out. Lefty Grove of the A's finally beat them 7-0. No National League team has even reached the 200 mark.

18.6 **D. St. Louis Cardinals**   The St. Louis Cardinals show two cardinals (birds, not players) perched on opposite ends of a bat. The Braves uniform shows a tomahawk, the Astros wear a star, and the Dodger uniform has no special display.

18.7 **C. Giants**   The New York Giants won four in a row

from 1921 through 1924, a record never equaled in the National League. The Yankees hold the major league record of five straight championships, which they accomplished twice: 1949-53 and 1960-64.

18.8   **B. Dodgers**   The Dodgers (Brooklyn and Los Angeles combined) have won a record total of 18 pennants (in 1916, 1920, 1941, 1947, 1949, 1952-53, 1955-56, 1959, 1963, 1965-66, 1974, 1977-78, 1981, 1988).

18.9   **C. 33**   They won first in 1921, and last in 1981. During this 61-year period, they won the American League pennant more than 54 percent of the time. (For details, see the next question.)

18.10 **D. 1950s**   They won eight in the 1950s: 1950-53, 1955-58. They won six in the 1920s, and five each in the 1930s, 1940s, and 1960s.

18.11 **C. 10**   Toronto hit them against Baltimore on September 14, 1987. Baltimore also hit 1 home run, and the two-team total of 11 also tied a record. The National League one-game, single-team record is 8, accomplished by Milwaukee (1953), Cincinnati (1956), San Francisco (1961), and Montreal (1978).

18.12 **A. Los Angeles Dodgers**   The Dodgers also showed a pretax profit margin of 25 percent in 1982—possibly a record in any sport, according to *The Wall Street Journal*. In terms of market value, Scully believed the team to be worth more than a quarter of a billion dollars.

18.13 **D. Al Kaline**   Al Kaline, an excellent hitter (lifetime .297) and defensive outfielder (10 Gold Glove awards), played for the Tigers in 2,834 games, from 1953-74. Cobb is a close second with 2,806, followed by Gehringer with 2,323.

18.14 **C. Willie Stargell**   Stargell played his entire 21-year career at Pittsburgh (1962-82), during which he had 475 home runs and 1,540 RBIs.

18.15 **B.** **extra-base hits** Gehrig edged Ruth by 1190 to 1189, counting only Ruth's extra-base hits as a Yankee. Ruth narrowly led Gehrig in the other categories: batting average, .349 to .340; runs, 1959 to 1888; and total bases, 5131 to 5059.

18.16 **D.** **Don Sutton** Sutton won 233 games as a Dodger, from 1966-80, before moving on to Houston as a free agent.

18.17 **D.** **Tommy Lasorda** Lasorda had been with the Dodgers since late 1976; 1990 was his 14th consecutive full season with them. In second place was Whitey Herzog of the Cardinals, who had been with them since 1980. Herzog resigned, however, midway through the 1990 season.

18.18 **D.** **all three** Chance managed the Cubs from 1905-12, Evers in 1913 and 1921, and Tinker in 1916. All three are in the Hall of Fame.

18.19 **B** **. 1965 Dodgers** The Dodger infield consisted of Wes Parker at first, Jim Lefebre at second, Jim Gilliam at third, and Maury Wills at shortstop.

18.20 **C.** **347** The New York Giants set the record in 1911. The American League record is 341, set by Oakland in 1976.

18.21 **B.** **Los Angeles Dodgers** The Dodgers do not wear pinstripes. The National League teams that do are Chicago, New York, Philadelphia, and San Diego.

18.22 **A.** **Johnny Bench** Bench hit 389 for the Reds, from 1967-83.

18.23 **A.** **Jimmy Foxx** Foxx hit 50 in 1938. Yastrzemski holds the Boston home run record for a lefthanded hitter, with 44 in 1967.

18.24 **C.** **Robin Roberts** Roberts appeared in 529 games, mostly as a starter, from 1948-61 (he later pitched for

Baltimore, Houston, and the Chicago Cubs). Carlton holds the Phillies record for games started, with 499 from 1972-86 (he also pitched for St. Louis from 1965-71, and for San Francisco, the Chicago White Sox, Cleveland, and Minnesota from 1986-87).

18.25 **B. Joe Morgan played more years for Cincinnati than for Houston.**   Morgan played 10 years for Houston (1963-71, 1980), but only 8 for Cincinnati (1972-79). Foster played 10-and-a-fraction years for Cincinnati and just four-and-a-fraction for New York. Rose played 18-plus years for Cincinnati and five for Philadelphia. And Robinson played 10 full years for Cincinnati and six for Baltimore.

Chapter 19

Series Standouts

Each year, the season culminates with the World Series, for which a distinct body of statistical records has been kept since the inception of the Series in 1903. Here's a look at some of the Fall Classic's classic facts and figures. (Answers and explanations begin on page 198.)

19.1 The World Series has been played between teams from the same city quite a few times. In which of these cities did this *never* happen?
A. Chicago
B. New York
C. Philadelphia
D. St. Louis

19.2 Prior to its current best-of-seven format, how was the World Series structured?
A. best of three
B. best of five
C. best of nine
D. double elimination tournament among the four top teams

19.3 Who was the first manager to win the World Series in both leagues?
A. Sparky Anderson
B. Yogi Berra
C. Joe McCarthy
D. It has never been done.

19.4 Based on 20 or more games, who holds the record for the highest lifetime World Series batting average?
A. Lou Brock
B. Lou Gehrig
C. Lou Piniella
D. Lou Whitaker

19.5 Lou Gehrig set a record for the highest slugging average ever in a World Series. What was it?
A. .527
B. .927
C. 1.327
D. 1.727

19.6 Babe Ruth and Lou Gehrig share the record for runs scored in a four-game World Series. How many runs did each score to set this record?
A. 3
B. 6
C. 9
D. 12

19.7 Who holds the career record for most runs scored in World Series competition?
A. Yogi Berra
B. Lou Gehrig
C. Mickey Mantle
D. Babe Ruth

19.8 Who pitched eight complete games in a row in World Series competition, winning all but the last one?
A. Whitey Ford
B. Bob Gibson
C. Jim "Catfish" Hunter
D. Christy Mathewson

19.9 What pitcher has the best undefeated World Series mark
(6-0), as well as the most All-Star Game wins, three
(against just one loss)?
   A. Jack Coombs
   B. Whitey Ford
   C. Lefty Gomez
   D. Catfish Hunter

19.10 What pitcher has the record for *losing* the most World
Series games?
   A. Joe Bush
   B. Whitey Ford
   C. Christy Mathewson
   D. Don Newcombe

19.11 Who pitched a complete game victory in the longest
World Series game in history?
   A. Bob Gibson
   B. Walter Johnson
   C. Christy Mathewson
   D. Babe Ruth

19.12 When was the first World Series night game?
   A. 1911
   B. 1931
   C. 1951
   D. 1971

19.13 What was the first year in which the World Series was
televised?
   A. 1937
   B. 1947
   C. 1957
   D. 1967

19.14 What is the individual record for the most World Series
played in?
   A. 5
   B. 8
   C. 11
   D. 14

19.15 What is the most games a complete World Series has
gone in which one team made no errors?
A. 4
B. 5
C. 6
D. 7

19.16 What is the most runs (all games combined) ever scored
by the losing team in a World Series?
A. 25
B. 35
C. 45
D. 55

19.17 Who appeared in more World Series than any other
player during the 1960s?
A. Orlando Cepeda
B. Al Downing
C. Roger Maris
D. Claude Osteen

19.18 How many umpires are used in a World Series game?
A. 4
B. 5
C. 6
D. 7

19.19 What team appeared in the most World Series during the
1980s?
A. Kansas City
B. Los Angeles
C. Oakland
D. St. Louis

19.20 The Yankees have won more World Series (22) than any
other team. But what team has *lost* the most World Series?
A. Cubs
B. Dodgers
C. Giants
D. Yankees

19.21 What is the most games a pitcher has ever appeared in during a seven-game World Series?
   A. 4
   B. 5
   C. 6
   D. 7

19.22 How many days did the San Francisco earthquake of 1989 delay the continuation of the Oakland-San Francisco World Series?
   A. 3
   B. 6
   C. 10
   D. 15

19.23 What pitcher holds the career record for hurling the most World Series shutouts?
   A. Whitey Ford
   B. Bob Gibson
   C. Christy Mathewson
   D. Babe Ruth

19.24 What effect did the owners' lockout at the start of the 1990 season have on the timing of the 1990 World Series?
   A. none
   B. Because of the season's late start, the World Series was pushed back three days.
   C. Because of the season's late start, the World Series was pushed back one week.
   D. Because of the season's late start, the World Series was pushed back 10 days.

19.25 Who was the only player to make the final out of a World Series by being caught trying to steal?
   A. Lou Brock
   B. Rickey Henderson
   C. Willie Mays
   D. Babe Ruth

Answers and Explanations

19.1 **C. Philadelphia**   Series within a city happened in
Chicago in 1906, in St. Louis in 1944 (the "Trolley
Series"), and in New York (including the borough of
Brooklyn) in 1921, 1922, 1923, 1936, 1937, 1941,
1947, 1949, 1951, 1952, 1953, 1955, and 1956 (the
"Subway Series").

19.2 **C. best of nine**   The last Series with the best-of-nine
format was 1921, when the New York Giants
defeated the New York Yankees 5 games to 3 in what
was also the first "Subway Series." The format was
best-of-nine in the first World Series in 1903, but
changed to a seven-game format in the second World
Series in 1905 (no Series was played in 1904). It
remained that way until 1919, the first of three
consecutive years in which the best-of-nine format
was resurrected. No best-of-nine World Series,
incidentally, ever went more than eight games.

19.3 **A. Sparky Anderson**   Anderson's Detroit team won
the Series in 1984; previously, his Cincinnati teams
won in 1975 and 1976. On June 15, 1990, he became
only the tenth manager ever to win 1,800 games, and
he is also the first manager to have won more than
800 games in each league (he won 863 with
Cincinnati from 1970-78, and should win his 1,000th
with Detroit in 1991).

19.4 **A. Lou Brock**   Brock, with St. Louis, hit .391 in 21
games (1964, 1967, 1968)—in all, 34 for 87. The
other players listed as answer choices had World
Series batting averages as follows: Gehrig, .361 in 34
games; Piniella, .319 in 22 games; and Whitaker, .278
in five games. The World Series batting leader among
players with 15 or more games, however, is Pepper
Martin, who hit .418 (23 for 55) in 15 games for the
Cardinals in 1928, 1931, and 1934.

19.5 **D. 1.727** In the four-game 1928 Series, for the Yankees against St. Louis, Gehrig went 6 for 11, including one double and four home runs. He also drew six walks, giving him an on-base percentage of .706. It was a rough Series for Cardinal pitchers: Gehrig's teammate Babe Ruth hit three home runs and slugged 1.375.

19.6 **C. 9** Ruth did it in 1928, and Gehrig in 1932. Reggie Jackson, who scored 10 runs for the Yankees in a six-game Series in 1977, is the only player ever to score more runs in one World Series.

19.7 **C. Mickey Mantle** Mantle scored a total of 42 times in 12 series, in 65 games from 1951-64. He also holds the record for the most lifetime World Series home runs, with 18.

19.8 **B. Bob Gibson** Gibson did it pitching for St. Louis in 1964 (2), 1967 (3), and 1968 (3). His seven wins in a row is also a World Series record.

19.9 **C. Lefty Gomez** Gomez achieved his record while pitching for the Yankees in 1932 and 1936-38. Coombs, pitching for the Philadelphia Athletics in 1910-11 and for Brooklyn in 1916, and Herb Pennock, pitching for the Yankees in 1923, 1926-27, and 1932, each had Series records of 5-0. Ford, pitching for the Yankees in 11 Series from 1950-64, is the all-time World Series win leader with 10.

19.10 **B. Whitey Ford** Ford lost 8 games to go with his 10 wins, pitching in 11 Series from 1950-64. Bush lost 5 in a row (for the Philadelphia Athletics in 1914, the Boston Red Sox in 1918, and the New York Yankees in 1922-23), but his lifetime World Series record was 2-5 (he was 1-0 for Philadelphia in 1913, and won once for the Yankees). Mathewson was 5-5 in World Series competition for the New York Giants (1905, 1911-13), with three shutouts in the 1905 Series. Newcombe lost only half as many World Series games as Ford, but has the dubious distinction of

having the most World Series losses (4) without a
victory.

19.11 **D. Babe Ruth**   Pitching for Boston, Ruth defeated
Sherry Smith of the Brooklyn Dodgers 2-1 in 14
innings on October 9, 1916. No one else, starter or
reliever, has ever pitched that many innings in a
single World Series game.

19.12 **D. 1971**   October 13, 1971, at Three Rivers Stadium in
Pittsburgh. The Pirates beat the Orioles 4-3. The first
night All-Star Game had taken place way back in
1943, and the first regular-season night game in 1935.

19.13 **B. 1947**   In the Series that year, the Yankees beat the
Dodgers 4 games to 3. The first televised regular
season baseball game had also involved the Dodgers:
On August 26, 1939, a Dodgers-Reds game was
televised from Ebbets Field in Brooklyn, by New
York station W2XBS.

19.14 **D. 14**   Yogi Berra played in 14 for the Yankees. In all,
he took part in 75 Series games, 65 of them
consecutive between 1947 and 1963.

19.15 **B. 5**   In 1937, the Yankees made no errors in a
five-game Series against the Giants. In a four-game
Series, Baltimore fielded perfectly in 1966 against
Los Angeles. Deservedly, both teams with 1.000
fielding percentages won the championship.

19.16 **D. 55**   This is also the record for *any* team—winner or
loser. The Yankees outscored the Pirates 55-27 in the
1960 World Series (the two teams' combined total of
81 is also a record), but lost 4 games to 3. In order,
with the Pirates' scores coming first, the games went:
6-4, 3-16, 0-10, 3-2, 5-2, 0-12, 10-9.

19.17 **C. Roger Maris**   Maris played in five for the Yankees
(1960-64) and two for St. Louis (1967-68). His
lifetime World Series average was only .217, but he
hit a career-high .385 in the 1967 Series.

19.18 **C. 6** Although regular season games use four umpires, World Series games use six—the extra ones standing well down each foul line, mainly to help rule on long fair-foul calls.

19.19 **D. St. Louis** St. Louis appeared in three, each of which went the full seven games. They defeated Milwaukee in 1982, lost to Kansas City in 1985, and lost to Minnesota in 1987. Teams that appeared in two World Series in the 1980s were Kansas City (1980 and 1985), Los Angeles (1981 and 1988), Oakland (1988 and 1989), and Philadelphia (1980 and 1983).

19.20 **B. Dodgers** The Dodgers have lost 12 (in 1916, 1920, 1941, 1947, 1949, 1952-53, 1956, 1966, 1974, and 1977-78). They were 1-8 in Brooklyn, but have a winning record of 5-4 in Los Angeles. The Yankees and Giants each have 11 losses, and the Cubs have 8.

19.21 **D. 7** Darold Knowles relieved in all seven games for Oakland against New York in 1973. In 6 1/3 innings, he was 0-0 with two saves, including a save in the deciding seventh game. Dan Quisenberry appeared for Kansas City in all six games of a six-game World Series in 1980, and Mike Marshall appeared for Los Angeles in all five games of a five-game World Series in 1974. No pitcher has ever appeared in all four games of a four-game World Series (if it's that one-sided, evidently, relief pitchers aren't needed all that much).

19.22 **C. 10** Cancellation of the Series was debated, but soon a consensus emerged that "the show must go on." One effect of the delay was to make it impossible for *The World Almanac* to include World Series results—for which they normally wait before going to the printer—in their 1990 edition.

19.23 **C. Christy Mathewson** Mathewson had four—three in the 1905 World Series and one in 1913. Ford had three (two in 1960, one in 1961), Gibson had two

(one each in 1967 and 1968), and Ruth had one in
1918.

19.24   **B.** **Because of the season's late start, the World Series
was pushed back three days.**   The Series opener
was rescheduled for October 16, three days later than
originally planned. As a result, it became the first
Series since 1984 to start on a Tuesday.

19.25   **D.** **Babe Ruth**   In 1926, in the seventh and deciding
game against the Cardinals, Ruth was thrown out
trying to steal second (by catcher Bob O'Farrell).

Chapter 20

Extra Innings

If a question was too tough to put in any of the other chapters, chances are it found its way into this one. Please consider this quiz your final exam. (Answers and explanations begin on page 210.)

20.1 When was the last time that a lefthanded catcher played in the major leagues?
- **A.** never
- **B.** 1900
- **C.** 1940
- **D.** 1980

20.2 All of these things have happened at least once in major league history. But which one had never happened until 1990?
- **A.** Three triples are hit in a game, twice in a season, by the same player.
- **B.** Three triples (the combined total for both teams) are hit in an All-Star Game.
- **C.** Two triple plays are made by the same team in a single game.
- **D.** Two triple steals are made by the same team in a single game.

20.3 Which of these feats has never been accomplished?
  A. A league's home run leader also has the fewest strikeouts by a regular player.
  B. A player hits for the cycle twice in a season.
  C. A player hits three or more home runs in a game three times in the same season.
  D. A pitcher hits two grand slams in one game.

20.4 What pitcher hit a home run in each of four consecutive games—a record for a pitcher?
  A. Ken Brett
  B. Tony Cloninger
  C. Don Drysdale
  D. Juan Marichal

20.5 The year after George Sisler got a record 257 hits, with a .420 average (in 1922), what happened to cause him to miss the next season and never again be as good a hitter?
  A. He broke a toe.
  B. He developed a bad sinus infection.
  C. He sat out a year because of a contract dispute.
  D. He was hit in the head with a pitch.

20.6 If a designated hitter is moved to a defensive position, and no other defensive change is made at the same time, what happens to the batting order?
  A. The DH bats in the same position as he did before, and a new DH must be brought into the game. The new DH bats in the position of the replaced defensive player.
  B. The DH bats in the same position as he did before, and the pitcher bats in the position of the replaced defensive player.
  C. The DH bats in the position of the replaced defensive player, and the pitcher bats in the position where the DH had been batting.
  D. The manager has the right to choose either B or C above.

20.7 In what current stadium is the distance from home plate
to the deepest point in centerfield the greatest?
A. Busch Stadium
B. Cleveland Stadium
C. Tiger Stadium
D. Yankee Stadium

20.8 What early star was the first player to get more than
3,000 major league hits in his career?
A. Cap Anson
B. Ty Cobb
C. Nap Lajoie
D. Wee Willie Keeler

20.9 What major league player was born on a train in the
Panama Canal Zone?
A. Juan Berenguer
B. Rod Carew
C. Ben Oglivie
D. Manny Sanguillen

20.10 Topps issued a special baseball card, supposedly one of a
kind, in 1990, but by August, three additional copies had
been found in packs, and were already being valued by
some experts at more than $10,000 each. Whose picture
is on the card?
A. George Bush
B. Bart Giamatti
C. Pete Rose
D. Sadaharu Oh

20.11 Through 1990, how many times did an arbitrator find
major league owners to be guilty of collusion (i.e.,
conspiring to keep down salaries of free agents, or of
players in general)?
A. 1
B. 2
C. 3
D. 6

20.12 Hall of Famer Earl Averill, the Indians' all-time home run
       leader, is known for all but which of the following?
       A. being the first American League player to hit a home
          run in his first major league at-bat
       B. breaking Dizzy Dean's toe (and bringing an end to
          Dean's career) by hitting a line drive in the 1937
          All-Star Game
       C. having the nickname "the Earl of Snohomish,"
          because of his home town
       D. hitting a home run off Rip Sewell's blooper pitch in
          the 1946 All-Star Game

20.13 What is JUGS?
       A. the best-selling pitching machine, made by a
          company of the same name
       B. slang for an umpire's chest protector
       C. a portable dugout dispenser for refrigerated liquids
          for players to drink during a game
       D. a riding machine used to rake and smooth out the
          infield before a game

20.14 In which decade did the most different pitchers have at
       least one season with 30 or more complete games?
       A. 1940s
       B. 1950s
       C. 1960s
       D. 1970s

20.15 Cal Hubbard made the Pro Football Hall of Fame in
       Canton, Ohio, as a star tackle in the National Football
       League, but he also made the Baseball Hall of
       Fame—making him the only person to be in both. What
       was his claim to fame in baseball?
       A. manager
       B. outfielder
       C. pitcher
       D. umpire

20.16 In determining on-base average, what is *not* included in
the players' outs?
A. reaching first because of a fielder's choice
B. reaching first on an error
C. sacrifice flies
D. sacrifices

20.17 The pennant-winning Cubs team of 1929 included all but
which of these Hall of Famers?
A. Kiki Cuyler
B. Rogers Hornsby
C. Chuck Klein
D. Hack Wilson

20.18 Who, along with pitcher Jimmy Ring, was traded for
player-manager Rogers Hornsby in December 1926?
A. Frankie Frisch
B. Babe Herman
C. George Sisler
D. Paul Waner

20.19 When Macmillan's *The Baseball Encyclopedia* went from
its seventh to its eighth edition, one hitter mysteriously
lost 12 hits—going from 3,430 to 3,418, and dropping
from sixth to seventh on the all-time hit list—and also
had his lifetime batting average drop from .329 to .327.
Who was this hitter?
A. Rod Carew
B. Eddie Collins
C. Tris Speaker
D. Honus Wagner

20.20 How many stitches are on a baseball?
A. 58
B. 108
C. 158
D. 208

20.21 Which of the following pitchers does *not* share a record for striking out six batters in an All-Star Game?
- **A.** Bob Feller
- **B.** Carl Hubbell
- **C.** Ferguson Jenkins
- **D.** Johnny Vander Meer

20.22 In 1984, in *The Hidden Game of Baseball*, Pete Palmer introduced the concept of "linear weights," in which values—both positive and negative—are assigned to different results a batter can get at the plate and on the base paths. A single, for example, is given a point value of .46 because it is likely, on the average, to produce .46 runs; and a home run is worth 1.40. Outs are assigned a negative value sufficient to make league totals for everything come out to zero. The value of making an out as a batter varies from year to year, but is usually around −.25. In this system, what values are assigned to stealing a base and to being thrown out trying to steal?
- **A.** .15 for stealing, −.25 for being thrown out trying to steal
- **B.** .30 for stealing, −.30 for being thrown out trying to steal
- **C.** .30 for stealing, −.60 for being thrown out trying to steal
- **D.** .60 for stealing, −.60 for being thrown out trying to steal

20.23 How is the statistic known as "isolated power" determined?
- **A.** by counting the number of games in which a player was the only one on his team with an extra-base hit
- **B.** by dividing a player's total home runs into the number of home runs he hit with no one on base
- **C.** by dividing the number of extra-base hits a player has by his total at-bats
- **D.** by subtracting a player's batting average from his slugging average

20.24 Whom did *The Sporting News* name "Player of the Decade" for the 1970s?

   A. Johnny Bench

   B. Jim Palmer

   C. Pete Rose

   D. Willie Stargell

20.25 Which of these records is understated—that is, which feat has been improved on in actual play?

   A. The most consecutive singles by a team in an inning is 10.

   B. The most consecutive doubles by a team in an inning is 5.

   C. The most consecutive triples by a team in an inning is 4.

   D. The most consecutive home runs by a team in an inning is 3.

Answers and Explanations

20.1 **D. 1980**   Mike Squires of the Chicago White Sox was the catcher. Normally a first baseman, where he won a Gold Glove award in 1981, he also played some third base in 1983 and 1984, making him the first lefthanded third baseman in the major leagues in more than 50 years.

20.2 **C. Two triple plays are made by the same team in a single game.**   The Minnesota Twins pulled off two triple plays for the first time in major league history in losing 1-0 to the Boston Red Sox at Fenway on July 18, 1990. Both were sharp grounders hit to third baseman Gary Gaetti, then relayed to second baseman Al Newman and to first baseman Kent Hrbek. Tom Brunansky hit into the first one in the fourth inning, with the bases loaded; Jody Reed hit into the second one in the eighth inning, with runners on first and second. Gary Gaetti, who started both triple plays in same game, had (after that game) started five of Twins' six previous triple plays, and been involved in six of the last seven.

 In 1905, David Brain hit three triples in a game twice in a season, playing for St. Louis (May 29) and Pittsburgh (August 8). Three triples were hit in the 1978 All-Star Game, two by Rod Carew in a losing cause, and one, the game-winning hit, by Steve Garvey in the ninth inning. On July 25, 1930, the Philadelphia Athletics had two triple steals against Cleveland—one in the first inning and one in the fourth. The latter involved future Hall of Famers Cochrane, Simmons and Foxx.

20.3 **C. A player hits three or more home runs in a game three times in the same season.**   Several players have had three-homer games *twice* in a season, though: Johnny Mize did it twice (1938 and 1940), and doing it once each were Ralph Kiner (1947), Ted Williams (1957), Willie Mays (1961), Willie Stargell

(1971), Dave Kingman (1979), Doug DeCinces (1982), and Joe Carter (1989).

The other three feats happened just once each. In 1945, Tommy Holmes (Boston) led the National League in both home runs (28) and fewest strikeouts (only 9). Babe Herman hit for the cycle twice for Brooklyn in 1931. Tony Cloninger, a pitcher, hit two grand slams for the Atlanta Braves on July 3, 1966.

20.4 **A.** **Ken Brett**   Brett did it for Philadelphia in 1973 (June 9, 13, 18, 23). In 14 years (1967, 1969-81), playing for Boston, Milwaukee, Philadelphia, Pittsburgh, the New York Yankees, the Chicago White Sox, California, Minnesota, Los Angeles, and Kansas City, Brett hit .262 with a .406 slugging average.

20.5 **B.** **He developed a bad sinus infection.**   The infection affected his optic nerve, and hence his eyesight. In those days, unfortunately, there were no antibiotics to help him.

20.6 **B.** **The DH bats in the same position as he did before, and the pitcher bats in the position of the replaced defensive player.**   Once a team moves its DH to a defensive position, it may not use a DH for the remainder of the game—that rules out choice A. Choices C and D are ruled out by the fact that the position in which the DH (or any other player) bats in the lineup cannot change.

20.7 **D.** **Tiger Stadium**   Tiger Stadium's centerfield fence is 440 feet from home plate. Old parks tended to have deeper centerfields than newer ones, and Tiger Stadium is the oldest park in the major leagues. Games have been played there since 1900, when it was known as Bennett Park. It became Navin Field in 1912, Briggs Stadium in 1938, and Tiger Stadium on January 1, 1961. The deepest centerfield in the National League is Busch Stadium in St. Louis, 414 feet.

20.8 **A. Cap Anson**   Playing for Chicago from 1876-97, Anson got 3,041 hits. From 1871-75, he also had 430 hits for the Rockford Forest Citys and Philadelphia Athletics of the National Association.

20.9 **B. Rod Carew**   The year was 1945. Berenguer, Oglivie, and Sanguillen were all born in Panama as well.

20.10 **A. George Bush**   The card depicts President George Bush, who played first base on Yale's varsity baseball team, in college uniform. Though it was supposed to be issued only to the president, a few extras—no one seems to know how many—were printed. Some dealers and collectors suspected that Topps had released the extra cards deliberately in an effort to pump up sales.

20.11 **C. 3**   First, arbitrator Thomas Roberts, whom owners tried to fire in 1986, but found they couldn't (due to another arbitrator's finding), created "new look" free agency in a 1987 ruling on a suit filed by Major League Baseball Players Association in 1986. Then in 1988, arbitrator George Nicolau found owners guilty in a second case, which had been filed in 1987. Finally, in 1990, Nicolau found owners guilty in a third case, which had been filed in 1988. As a result of the rulings, a number of new players were granted free agent status.

20.12 **D. hitting a home run off Rip Sewell's blooper pitch in the 1946 All-Star Game**   It was Ted Williams who hit the home run off the blooper pitch in the 1946 All-Star Game. Williams also had another homer and two other hits, as the American League won 12-0.

20.13 **A. the best-selling pitching machine, made by a company of the same name**   For about $3,000, you can get one complete with automatic ball feeder and batting cage.

20.14 **D. 1970s**   Ferguson Jenkins (1971), Steve Carlton

(1972), and Jim Hunter (1975) each had one season
with exactly 30 complete games. In the 1940s, Bob
Feller had 36 in 1946, and Dizzy Trout (Detroit) had
33 in 1944. In the 1950s, Robin Roberts had 33 in
1953 and 30 in 1952. Juan Marichal, with exactly 30
complete games in 1968, was the only pitcher to
reach that level during the entire decade. In the
1980s, no one had more complete games than Rick
Langford (Oakland), who had 28 in 1980.

20.15 **D.** **umpire** An American League umpire from
1937-51, and a supervisor of American League
umpires for 15 more years, Hubbard was the first
umpire to throw a pitcher out of a game for throwing
a spitball (Nels Potter of St, Louis, in 1944). In the
NFL, he played for championship teams in New York
(1927) and Green Bay (1931-33). He's also in the
College Football Hall of Fame (he played at
Centenary and Geneva).

20.16 **D.** **sacrifices** Statistics expert Pete Palmer refuses to
count sacrifice flies as outs, either, since they are not
counted as outs in determining batting average.

20.17 **C.** **Chuck Klein** Klein played for the Phillies that year,
batting .356 and leading the league with 43 home
runs. Cuyler, Hornsby, and Wilson batted .360, .380,
and .345, respectively, that year, with Hornsby and
Wilson each hitting 39 home runs (Cuyler had 15).

20.18 **A.** **Frankie Frisch** Frisch and Ring went from the
Giants to the Cardinals in exchange for Hornsby.

20.19 **D.** **Honus Wagner** No clear explanation as to whether
the changes were purposeful or accidental was
immediately forthcoming from Macmillan. The
computer that made the calculations may have been
correcting a previous error, or it may have been
subject to a keypunch inputting error. Such things can
be very hard to prove or disprove by looking through
original box scores, since some of them may no
longer exist.

20.20 **B. 108**   This has been true since the last century. Balls also have a cushioned cork center (introduced in 1931), then are wound in wool and cotton, cemented, covered (see question 1.1) and stitched.

20.21 **A. Bob Feller**   The others listed as choices all did accomplish the feat: Hubbell in three innings on July 10, 1934, Vander Meer in 2 2/3 innings on July 13, 1943, and Jenkins in three innings on July 11, 1967. Larry Jansen also did it, in five innings, on July 11, 1950 (nowadays, pitchers are limited to three innings, except in extra-inning games).

20.22 **C. .30 for stealing,–.60 for being thrown out trying to steal**   Making an out by being caught stealing is much more costly to a team, on the average, than making an out as a batter. According to the formula and the theory behind it, a player who is successful at stealing fewer than two out of three times would help his team more by not trying to steal any bases at all.
    Other values in the linear weights system, by the way, are .80 for a double, 1.02 for a triple, and .33 for reaching first via a walk or being hit by a pitch. Linear weights are an attempt to give an accurate picture of how many extra runs a player helped his team score, compared with the league average.

20.23 **D. by subtracting a player's batting average from his slugging average**   This is equivalent to subtracting the player's hits from his total bases, and then dividing by his at-bats. The statistic can be found in such books as *Total Baseball*, by John Thorn and Pete Palmer. The three best single-season totals for isolated power (and nine of the top 14) all belong to Babe Ruth (.472 in 1920, .469 in 1921, and .417 in 1927). Lou Gehrig's 1927 season produced the next best total of .392.

20.24 **C. Pete Rose**   From 1970-79, Rose hit .300 every year except 1974, and collected a total of 2,045 hits. Bench led the decade in RBIs (1,013), Palmer led in

wins (186) and ERA (2.61), and Stargell led in home
runs (296).

20.25 **D. The most consecutive home runs by a team in an
inning is 3.**   The most consecutive home runs in an
inning is 4, and it has been done more than once: by
Milwaukee against Cincinnati on June 8, 1961,
seventh inning; by Cleveland against Los Angeles,
July 31, 1963, second game, sixth inning; and by
Minnesota against Kansas City on May 2, 1964, in
the 11th inning.
   The record for consecutive doubles is five
(Washington vs. Boston, June 9, 1934, eighth inning);
the most consecutive triples record is four (Boston vs.
Detroit, May 6, 1934, fourth inning); and the most
consecutive singles record is 10 (St. Louis vs.
Boston, National League, September 17, 1920, fourth
inning). Ten is also the record for the most
consecutive hits in an inning.

Bibliography

Hundreds of books about baseball are in print, and hundreds of older titles can be found at large libraries. The following list contains a sampling of mostly recent titles that are particularly important or that the author believes will interest readers of this book.

Allen, Maury. *Baseball: The Lives Behind the Seams.* New York: Macmillan Publishing Co., 1990.

The 1990 American League Red Book—1990. St. Louis: The Sporting News Publishing Co., 1990.

Angell, Roger. *Late Innings: A Baseball Companion.* New York: Ballantine Books, 1982.

Asinof, Eliot. *Eight Men Out.* New York: Henry Holt and Co., 1987.

Beckett, James. *Sport Americana Baseball Card Price Guide, No. 12.* Cleveland, Ohio: Edgewater Book Co., 1990.

Benson, Michael. *Ballparks of North America: A Comprehensive Historical Reference to Grounds, Yards & Stadiums.* Jefferson, North Carolina: McFarland & Co., 1989.

Berger, Sy, Frank Slocum, and Red Foley. *The Complete Picture Collection: Topps Baseball Cards, A 40 Year History.* New York: Warner Books Inc., 1990.

Berkow, Ira. *Pitchers Do Get Lonely: And Other Sports Stories.* New York: Macmillan Publishing Co., 1988.

Berra, Yogi with Tom Horton. *Yogi: It Ain't Over...* New York: Harper & Row, 1989.

Bouton, Jim. *Ball Four.* 20th anniv. rev. ed. New York: Macmillan Publishing Co., 1990.

Brosnan, Jim. *The Long Season.* New York: Penguin Books, 1983.

Bryson, Michael G. *The Twenty-Four-Inch Home Run: And Other Outlandish, Incredible but True Events in Baseball History.* Chicago: Contemporary Books, 1990.

Carter, Craig, ed. *The Complete Baseball Record Book 1990.* St. Louis: The Sporting News Publishing Co., 1990.

Coberly, Rich. *The No-Hit Hall of Fame: No-Hitters of the Twentieth Century.* Newport Beach, California: Triple Play Publications, 1985.

Creamer, Robert W. *Babe: The Legend Comes to Life.* New York: Simon & Schuster, 1974.

Creamer, Robert. *Stengel: His Life & Times.* New York: Dell Publishing Co., 1985.

Dorfman, H.A. & Karl Kuehl. *The Mental Game of Baseball: A Guide to Peak Performance.* Notre Dame, Indiana: Diamond Communications, 1989.

Eckes, Dennis and Jack Smalling. *Sport Americana Baseball Address List.* Lakewood, Ohio: Edgewater Book Co., 1986.

Einstein, Charles, ed. *The Baseball Reader: Favorites from Fireside Books of Baseball.* New York: McGraw Hill, 1980.

Einstein, Charles, ed. *The Fireside Book of Baseball.* 4th ed. New York: Simon & Schuster, 1987.

Fleming, G.H. *The Unforgettable Season.* New York: Penguin Books, 1982.

Florence, Gene. *The Standard Baseball Card Price Guide.* rev. 3rd ed. Paducah, Kentucky: Collector Books, 1991.

Golenbock, Peter. *Dynasty: The New York Yankees 1949-64.* New York: Berkley Publishing Group, 1985.

Hoppel, Joe and Craig Carter, eds. *Baseball Trivia 2.* St. Louis: The Sporting News Publishing Co., 1987.

James, Bill. *The Bill James Historical Abstract.* New York. Random House, 1988.

James, Bill. *The Bill James Baseball Abstract.* New York: Ballantine, 1987.

James, Bill, Don Zminda and Project Scoresheet. *The Great American Baseball Stat Book.* New York: Villard Books, 1988.

Jackson, Reggie and Mike Lupica. *Reggie.* New York: Random House, 1984.

Kahn, Roger. *The Boys of Summer.* New York: Harper & Row, 1987.

Kronick, Buck. *The Baseball Fan's Complete Guide to Collecting Autographs.* Crozet, Virginia: Betterway Publications, 1990.

LaSorda, Tommy & David Fisher. *The Artful Dodger.* New York: Avon Books, 1986.

Lau, Charley and Alfred Glassbrenner. *The Winning Hitter: How to Play Championship Baseball.* New York: William Morrow & Co., 1984.

Lehmann-Haupt, Christopher. *Me & DiMaggio: A Baseball Fan Goes in Search of His Gods.* New York: Simon & Schuster, 1986.

Levine, Peter, ed. *Baseball History: An Annual of Original Baseball Research.* Westport, Connecticut: Meckler Books, 1989.

Luciano, Ron & David Fisher. *Remembrances of Swings Past.* New York: Bantam Books, 1981.

Mann, Steve and Ken Mallin. *The Sporting News Rotisserie & Fantasy League Guide.* St. Louis: The Sporting News Publishing Co., 1990.

McCarver, Tim and Ray Robinson. *Oh, Baby I Love It.* New York: Random House, 1987.

The National League Green Book—1990. St. Louis: The Sporting News Publishing Co., 1990.

Neft, David S. and Richard M. Cohen. *The Sports Encyclopedia: Baseball, 1988 Edition.* New York. St. Martin's Press, 1988.

Neft, David and Richard M. Cohen. *The World Series.* New York: St. Martin's Press, 1990.

Nemec, David. *Great Baseball Feats, Facts & Firsts.* New York: Signet, 1988.

Nash, Bruce and Allan Zullo. *The Baseball Hall of Shame.* 3 vols. Pocket Books, 1986.

Official Baseball Rules. St. Louis: The Sporting News Publishing Co., 1988.

Okrent, Daniel and Harris Lewine, eds. *The Ultimate Baseball Book.* Boston: Houghton Mifflin, 1988.

Okrent, Daniel and Steve Wulf. *Baseball Anecdotes.* New York: Harper & Row, 1989.

Peary, Danny, ed. *Cult Baseball Players: The Greats, the Flakes, the Weird, and the Wonderful.* New York: Simon & Schuster, 1990.

Peterson, Robert. *Only the Ball Was White: A History of Legendary Black Players and All-Black Professional Teams Before Black Men Played in the Major Leagues.* New York: McGraw Hill, 1984.

Petroff, Tom with Jack Clary. *Baseball Signs and Signals.* Dallas: Taylor Publishing Co., 1987.

Reichler, Joseph L., ed. *The Baseball Encyclopedia: The Complete and Official Record of Major League Baseball.* 7th rev. & exp. ed. New York: Macmillan Publishing Co., 1988.

Reidenbaugh, Lowell and Craig Carter. *Take Me Out to the Ball Park.* St. Louis: The Sporting News Publishing Co., 1987.

Ritter, Lawrence S. *The Glory of Their Times: The Story of the Early Days of Baseball Told by the Men Who Played It.* New York: Random House, 1985.

Shatzkin, Mike, ed. *The Ballplayers: Baseball's Ultimate Biographical Reference.* New York: Arbor House, 1990.

Siwoff, Seymour, the Hirdt brothers, et. al. *The Elias Baseball Analyst.* New York: Macmillan Publishing Co., 1990.

The Sporting News Baseball Guide. St. Louis: The Sporting News Publishing Co., 1990.

The Sporting News Official Baseball Register. St. Louis: The Sporting News Publishing Co., 1990.

Sporting News Baseball Trivia II. St. Louis: The Sporting News Publishing Co., 1987.

Sports Collectors Digest. *Baseball Card Price Guide.* 4th ed. Iola, Wisconsin: Krause Publications, 1990.

Sugar, Bert Randolph, ed. *Baseballistics.* New York: St. Martin's Press, 1990.

Thayer, Ernest L. *Casey at the Bat: A Ballad of the Republic, Sung in the Year 1888.* Putnam Publishing Group, 1980.

Thorn, John and Bob Carroll with David Reuther. *The Whole Baseball Catalogue: The Ultimate Guide to the Baseball Marketplace.* New York: Simon & Schuster, 1990.

Thorn, John, and Pete Palmer, eds. *Total Baseball: The Most Comprehensive Baseball Book Ever With Revolutionary New Statistics & Authoritative Essays on All Aspects of the Game.* New York: Warner Books Inc., 1989.

Thorn, John, and Pete Palmer, eds. *Total Baseball: 1990 Update.* New York: Warner Books Inc., 1990.

Baseball America's 1990 Directory. Durham, North Carolina: American Sports Publishing Inc., 1989.

Thorn, John et. al. *The Armchair Books of Baseball.* 2 vols. New York: Scribner, 1985.

Uecker, Bob with Mickey Herskowitz. *Catcher in the Wry.* New York: Jove Publications, 1987.

Veeck, Bill with Ed Linn. *Veeck as in Wreck.* New York: Fireside Books, 1989.

Waggoner, Glen, Kathleen Moloney, and Hugh Howard. *Baseball by the Rules: Pine Tar, Spitballs, and Midgets: An Anecdotal Guide to America's Oldest & Most Complex Sport.* New York: Prentice Hall Press, 1990.

Waggoner, Glen and Robert Sklar, ed. *Rotisserie League Baseball: The Official Rulebook and Complete Guide to Player Values.* rev. edn. New York: Bantam Books, 1990.

Will, George F. *Men at Work: The Craft of Baseball.* New York: Macmillan Publishing Co., 1990.

Index

Note: Teams are listed by city and identified by league (or name, when necessary to avoid ambiguity). Leagues are abbreviated as follows: AA, American Association; AL, American League; FL, Federal League; INT, International League; NA, National Association; NL, National League.